KATHARINE
HEPBURN

KATHARINE HEPBURN

Barbara Holland

—◆—

A Balliett & Fitzgerald Book

PARK LANE

NEW YORK

This 1998 edition is published by Park Lane Press,
a division of Random House Value Publishing, Inc.,
a Random House Company
201 East 50th Street, New York, New York 10022

A&E's acclaimed BIOGRAPHY series is available on videocassette from
A&E Home Video. Call 1-800-423-1212 to order.

A&E and **BIOGRAPHY** are trademarks of A&E Television Networks,
registered in the United States and other countries.

Park Lane Press and colophon are trademarks of
Random House Value Publishing, Inc.

Random House, Inc.
New York • Toronto • London • Sydney • Auckland
www.randomhouse.com

Printed and bound in the United States of America

A Balliett & Fitzgerald Book
Series Editor: Thomas Dyja
Book Design: Lisa Govan, Susan Canavan
Production Editors: Maria Fernandez, Mike Walters
Photo Research: Maria Fernandez
Assistant Editor: Irene Agriodimas

Library of Congress Cataloging-in-Publication Data

Holland, Barbara.
    Katharine Hepburn / Barbara Holland.   —1st ed.
            p.   cm.   —(Biography)
    "A Balliett & Fitzgerald book."
        Includes bibliographical (p. 171) references and index.
        1. Hepburn, Katharine, 1907–. 2. Motion picture actors and actresses—
United States—Biography.
    I. Title.   II. Series: Biography (Park Lane Press)
    PN2287.H45H66   1998
    791.43.028—dc21
    (B)   98-18840
                                                                  CIP

    ISBN 0-517-20097-X
    10 9 8 7 6 5 4 3 2 1
    First Edition

CONTENTS

circa 1959

CHAPTER ONE

WHERE SHE CAME FROM

She was always more than an actress. More than a celebrity. To several generations, she was a hero.

For girls growing up in the 1930s, '40s, and '50s, when a girl's only permissible ambition was housewifery, she held out hope. She showed them that a woman could be brave and strong, have adventures, and even talk back to a man without being punished for it.

It was a heady, subversive message. Girls were brought up to believe that a woman who went out in the man's world to forge her own destiny would be a coarse and vulgar creature, hard and mannish, scorned alike by men and other women. But there was Katharine Hepburn on the screen, proving that a woman could be every inch a lady but a fighter just the same. She could take risks. She could be a professional athlete, journalist, traveler, missionary, pilot, lawyer. And she could be happy in this wider world and still find a man to love her.

Even after women had shed their aprons, her guiding star went on shining. In 1984, when she was seventy-seven years old, 4,500 teenagers were asked to name their top ten living heroes; in the final tally, Hepburn was the only woman on the list, narrowly edging out the pope.

Was she a great actress? She won a record-breaking four Academy Awards for Best Actress, but in any role, she always seemed uniquely, compellingly herself, more life force than play actor. She herself shrugged acting off as a minor art form and once told a critic, "Never forget that they don't give a Nobel Prize for it, and that Shirley Temple was doing it perfectly adequately at the age of four."

Her movies seemed to be less about acting than about being Katharine Hepburn. As she admitted, "I was always playing myself in the movies, at least facets of myself." To be unable to be anyone except yourself is considered by some a serious flaw in an actress, but to criticize her acting is beside the point. She was a classic, an original. She could no more pretend to be someone else than Lake Superior could pretend to be the World Trade Center.

Nobody thought of her as a Hollywood star. However much time she spent in California, she was always a Connecticut Yankee. She always seemed just absent on leave from a more rigorous world, a world where people jump out of bed before dawn and plunge into ice-cold showers. She wore the air of a quintessential New England WASP, with its attendant code of loyalty, stoicism, dignity, nerves of steel, and grace under pressure; an exotic bloom indeed in the glamorously self-indulgent world of Hollywood in the 1930s and '40s.

The world she carried with her was the world she inherited

from her parents. American celebrities, especially in the entertainment world, rarely seem to have parents at all—it's as if they have sprung up full-grown from the collective unconscious, as isolated from the earth as the stars they're compared to. They have famous careers and love affairs and scandals, but they have no original home, no family. Nobody knows or cares who their parents were; even the stars themselves may have forgotten. Katharine Hepburn, however, came from a specific place and specific people and never really left them.

❖ ❖ ❖

"... compared to my mother and father, I'm dull."

The word that was used was "background." Snobs called it "breeding." It was what was meant when people said, as they often did, that Hepburn had "good bones." Good bones were inherited. You couldn't acquire them with makeup or camera angles. They came from your family, and Hepburn's family was deeply imbedded in her life.

She told an interviewer, late in her life, "I've had a pretty remarkable life, but compared to my mother and father, I'm dull. . . . The single most important thing anyone needs to know about me is that I am totally, completely the product of two damn fascinating individuals who happened to be my parents."

She remembered them always with love and gratitude, and in her memoir, *Me: Stories of My Life*, she insists over and over again that they were perfect people, perfect parents, and that she has always been the luckiest person on earth to have had them. This is refreshing in an age when whining has been elevated to a fine art, but such insistence seems almost suspicious. Is she hiding something from us, or, more likely, from herself? Were they maybe less than perfect? Just who were those fascinating people who jointly produced an American legend?

Katharine Hepburn's mother was born Katharine Houghton, and the Houghtons were a substantial clan. The Houghtons made money, but they made it respectably. They gave the world, among other gifts, the Houghton Mifflin publishing firm and Corning Glass Works; they developed the first lightbulb designed to hold Thomas Edison's invention. There were Houghton ambassadors and congressmen. There is Harvard's Houghton Library. Houghton ancestors had come to England with William the Conqueror; the first American Houghton came to New England in 1680. Our Katharine Hepburn and all five of her brothers and sisters were given "Houghton" as a middle name—it was that kind of family.

To be born among them should have been, at the very least, a promise of security, but fate had other plans for young Kit Houghton. She was the eldest of the three daughters of Alfred and Caroline Houghton, and they lived in a house on Lake Erie in West Hamburg, a fashionable summer retreat near Buffalo, New York. Caroline was an ambitious woman, a founder of political discussion groups and busy in the temperance movement. Forbidden to go to college herself, she was determined her daughters should be educated and independent women. Alfred Houghton, Kit's father, was vice president of Buffalo Scale, a solid citizen, prosperous and respected, but subject all his life to devastating spells of depression.

In 1892, when Alfred was suffering a prolonged bout of

gloom that interfered with his work, his older brother, Amory, the dictatorial head of Corning Glass, carried him back to his own home in Corning, New York, to recover his spirits. Instead of recovering, Alfred slipped away one afternoon and shot himself on a railroad track in a lumberyard.

In those days, suicide was a black mark against a family's good name. It was thought to mean an inherited nervous weakness, a form of madness that would trickle down through the generations. Presumably nobody would want to marry into such a family. Caroline urged her young daughters to keep the matter a secret, and they never mentioned, even in private, what had happened to their father. The notion of suicide as hereditary is considered absurd today, but paging through the family history, it's hard not to see it as a lingering Houghton family curse.

Caroline was left a widow with Kit, age fourteen; Edith, twelve; and Marion, nine. She hadn't given up the hope of a college education for them, but there was very little money, and she was at the mercy of her brother-in-law, Amory. She sold him the house and farm. She disposed of the horse and carriage and everything else saleable and gave Amory the money to invest for her, moving herself and the girls to rented quarters in Buffalo. Amory doled out a small allowance.

She never told her brother-in-law what the investments were earmarked for. Amory Houghton, like many men at the time, felt that higher education for women was a waste of good college space.

Having heard splendid reports of M. Carey Thomas, a remarkable woman who was president of Bryn Mawr college for women in Pennsylvania, Caroline was determined that her daughters would go there. However, their education had been private and distinctly spotty, and they hadn't a chance of passing Bryn Mawr's rigorous entrance examinations. First they would need to go to Miss Baldwin's School, which was near the college, to be prepped for it. Caroline planned to move to the area, where the four of them could save money by living together.

Without discussing the matter with Amory, she took Kit with her on a trip to Pennsylvania, where they visited the college, reserved three places at Miss Baldwin's, and rented a small house for the coming fall.

Then Caroline was diagnosed with inoperable stomach cancer. She wrote a will, hoping to ensure that her wishes for the girls would be respected. Trying to dodge her high-handed brother-in-law, she appointed no guardian for them.

Caroline Houghton died in September 1894, less than two years after her husband. Her stoical family never speculated on how she felt, knowing she was dying and leaving such young daughters orphaned in an untender world. Just before she died, she begged young Kit, then sixteen, to make sure that she and her sisters carried out the Bryn Mawr plan. Kit remembered her mother's wish as "a divine command."

Amory, however, did not.

He took charge at once, ignoring Caroline's will, and sent the girls to live with Caroline's cousin, Mack Smith, in Canandaigua, New York. Smith was delighted with the idea, since he planned to charge the estate every penny he could for the girls' upkeep. Cousin Mack itemized amounts as small as a penny, accounting for every button, every spool of thread; he even charged the girls for hot water for bathing. Kit kept herself and her sisters separate from the household, huddling with them in her own room. She read to them and reminded them of their background, so different from the grasping, unimaginative Smiths.

Somehow she persuaded her uncle Amory to let her take the

Bryn Mawr entrance exams without any preparatory schooling. No doubt he knew she would fail, and she did. But she came back still determined and used her slender allowance to hire tutors. Amory objected. College, he told her, made women unmarriageable. Apparently he concurred with his era's medical thinking, which held that educated females suffered from everything from anemia to madness, and that mental effort drew their blood supply into their brains, starving their ovaries and leaving them sterile. He might send her and her sisters to finishing school, but college was not an option.

Kit, however, did some eavesdropping and learned that under the terms of her mother's will, Amory was not their guardian. Now seventeen, she could choose one herself, according to law. She announced in court that she was appointing a lawyer acquaintance known to be in favor of education for women. Amory, outfoxed, caved in. She could go to Bryn Mawr—if she could get in.

Kit crammed tirelessly. When she went to take the exams, Amory went with her. He ran her around till midnight, wore her out, and made sure she got hardly any sleep—but she passed. Barely. She was admitted on probation, but she was admitted. Edith and Marion entered Miss Baldwin's School. Kit had kept her final promise to her mother.

After having struggled so hard to get in, at Bryn Mawr Kit relaxed and went a bit wild. She sneaked out at night to smoke cigarettes behind the tombstones in a cemetery. She careened around on horseback, riding astride, with her beloved sister Edith, scandalizing the neighborhood and earning herself a reprimand from the college. She ran up outrageous bills and earned a much harsher reprimand from Uncle Amory.

Uncle Amory, however, had other problems to cope with at the time. His younger brother Charlie, Kit's uncle, shot himself in March 1897 at Amory's own Corning Glass Works. It was the family's second suicide.

When Edith joined Kit at Bryn Mawr, alarms went off. Whenever there was a campus brawl, Edith Houghton was at its heart. She roomed with Kit, of course, and their rooms became the social center of the college.

In her sophomore year, Edith went too far. During the traditional riotous high jinks of the school's Lantern Night, she and some cronies broke into a dorm room and kidnapped a couple of terrified freshman girls, dragged them out half naked into the chilly woods, tied them to a tree, and left them there. The girls suffered no damage, but Edith, clearly the ringleader, was suspended and banished from campus. Notified of his niece's disgrace, Amory Houghton declared that her sentence was too light and that she should have been shot.

But nothing daunted Edith. After a month's suspension, she came back to her classes and promptly caught up with and passed the other students. She threw herself into every campus activity. She appeared in every play, but she set aside her acting ambitions. Deciding to become a doctor instead, she worked hard to enter Johns Hopkins Medical School in Baltimore, the only medical school in the country that accepted women.

Kit Houghton spent an extra year at Bryn Mawr, mostly to stay with Edith but partly because she didn't know what to do next. Her mother's vision had stopped short at college. What sort of life would a woman make for herself afterward? Going back to live with Uncle Amory in Corning would be a dreadful anticlimax, but what else could she do?

Kit went to Radcliffe to do extra work in chemistry and mathematics, thinking perhaps she too would try for Hopkins, where she and Edith could be together. For a few months, however, Edith was tempted by the theater again and went to

Kit Hepburn, Katharine's mother, in her later years.

Paris to study acting. By the time she came back to Hopkins, ready to work harder than ever, Kit had canceled her own vague thoughts of a medical career.

Kit and a friend went to Europe—Kit arriving with only ten dollars in her pocket—and toured the art museums. Always reckless with money, when her allowance came she went to Monte Carlo and lost it all, then won it back at roulette, along with enough extra to pay for her passage home.

Back home but still homeless, still without plans, Kit visited around rather than go to Amory, staying with anyone who invited her.

In February of 1903 she turned twenty-five, a ripe age for an unmarried woman at the time. She longed to fall in love, but nobody quite came up to her standards.

Then, visiting Edith at Johns Hopkins, she saw Tom Hepburn practicing fencing. He wore a white padded fencing jacket and white trousers, and he was, Kit told Edith later, the most beautiful creature she'd ever seen.

➤ ➤ ➤

"More of a sitter
than a suitor"

Norval Thomas Hepburn was two years younger than Kit. Through the Hepburns he could trace his ancestry back to the fourth Earl of Bothwell, third husband of Mary Queen of Scots and a thoroughly disagreeable fellow. On his mother's side he was a Powell, a distinguished Virginia name, as his mother, Nina, constantly reminded people. Her family had lost its fortune and vast plantations in the Civil War, and she spoke feelingly of Yankee pillage and butchery. Tom's father, the Reverend Sewell S. Hepburn, was an Episcopal minister known as "Parson Hep" who traveled a circuit of poor rural churches both black and white in Virginia and Maryland.

Parson Hep never made quite enough money. Nina had to take in boarders, sell eggs and butter, and make the whole family's clothes. She pushed her children hard to succeed, to put the family back on the map, to be handsome, brave, athletic, and prosperous. Impeccably mannered even in poverty, she always addressed her husband as "Reverend Hepburn," reportedly even in bed.

Young Tom adored his mother. He resented his father for their poverty, and for his mother's difficult life, which is probably why he left the church as a teenager and always spoke of religion as bunk. He admired his mother for her disciplined self-control. Self-control became his obsession.

Tom's older brothers, Charlie, Sewell Jr., and Lloyd, had all contracted venereal diseases from sowing their youthful wild oats among women outside their own social circle. It was the custom of the times, but young Tom disapproved. He vowed never to let sexual impulses boss him around, and he never did. Whatever the struggle, he stayed chaste. While he and Kit were courting, she kept hoping he would at least kiss her good night. He never did.

All his life Tom Hepburn started every day, winter and summer, with an ice-cold shower, a tradition that his daughter Katharine faithfully followed.

Many years later, in his sixties, when he fell ill he refused to see a doctor or say what was the matter with him, though as a doctor himself he would certainly have known. He was in excruciating pain, and it was finally discovered that his gall bladder had burst and his abdomen was packed hard with gallstones and bile, poisoning him. His daughter Kate remembered the episode with pride, writing that "he found moaning about one's health totally disgusting," perhaps an odd attitude in a doctor.

Dr. Tom was not an easy man. Still, the minute she first saw him, Kit Houghton wanted him badly. She took a job teaching school so she could stay in Baltimore and court the twenty-two-year-old medical student.

Her sister Edith disapproved. She thought Tom was conceited and arrogant and a snob. She preferred another classmate, Donald Hooker. The three of them were thrown into companionship through the alphabetical seating arrangements—destiny hangs by slender threads.

Tom was indeed striking, with blue eyes, mahogany-red hair, and chiseled features. In his Hopkins graduation picture he looks intense, leaning aggressively toward the camera, about to pounce. He had been a fullback at Randolph-Macon College and was always to be a competitive, rigorous athlete. He believed in physical competition as a kind of essential moral exercise.

What he didn't believe in, apparently, was love. Kit's courtship of him was discouraging. She told Edith he was "more of a sitter than a suitor." Finally, when he was telling her about his plans to study surgery at Heidelberg in Germany, she goaded him by saying that nothing, even marriage to other people, would interfere with their friendship. Astonished, Tom snapped, "If I don't marry you, I shall never marry anyone." His idea, no doubt, of a flowery proposal. Tom couldn't afford marriage, but luckily that fall the youngest Houghton sister, Marion, turned twenty-one, and Kit finally came into the inheritance Amory had been guarding—minus, of course, Cousin Mack's itemized bills for buttons and bathwater.

Tom and Kit were married at Shepherd's Delight, Hep and Nina Hepburn's farm in Maryland. As a bride, Kit wore black, to signify the death of the restless, ambitious girl in preparation for the rebirth of the devoted wife. Her new mother-in-law was scandalized. It confirmed her worst fears about the wicked, unprincipled Yankees.

If Kit couldn't share her feelings, troubles, and memories with the spartan Dr. Tom, sharing a bed was no problem. The couple were almost brazenly happy sexually, all through their marriage. Apparently it was quite noticeable across a crowded room; certainly their children were always aware of it.

AUNT EDITH

The most eccentric and dramatic of Katharine Hepburn's relatives was her aunt, Kit's next-younger sister Edith. A strong personal influence on her niece, she was the one who encouraged Kate to be an actress. Kate would base her performance of Jo in *Little Women* on her reckless, indomitable aunt.

Edith was gaunt and bony and wild, with long arms and legs, and she dressed at the far end of casual, in floppy, raggedy shirts and pants. She herself had wanted to be an actress. At Miss Baldwin's School she made her mark playing male roles in school plays, most notably the handsome soldier in *The Heart of the Princess Asra*, and at Bryn Mawr she was always onstage.

The star of Bryn Mawr's basketball team, Edith was also an ace gymnast, a chess whiz, and a brilliant science student, though she tended to break things in the lab. Her temper was famous, too.

After working hard to be accepted at Johns Hopkins Medical School, defying her era's prejudices against women doctors, Edith married her classmate Donald Hooker and dropped out of med school, with only one semester left to go. As a third-year medical student working in clinics, Edith had been horrified by the prevalence of venereal disease. Hooker, like Edith, was interested in venereal disease and accepted a fellowship to study with two distinguished genitourinary specialists in Germany. Edith knew that if she stayed in Baltimore to finish her course work, she would miss the chance to share the experience. From her work with venereal disease patients, it was an easy step for Edith to become involved in the fight for women's suffrage. Not until women got the vote would the brothels, which were riddled with syphilis and protected by the male establishment, be closed.

Edith's new interest soon drew in her older sister, Kit, as well. Within a few years Kit was following in Edith's footsteps, and her own world was suddenly quite the opposite of the quiet domesticity she had expected when she married Tom Hepburn.

And because of it her oldest daughter, Kate, would grow up center stage of the major struggle of the time, accustomed to the limelight, to cheers and jeers and hazing, before she was ten.

When they got back from his fellowship in Heidelberg, Kit was pregnant and it was time to choose a hospital for his internship. It was a delicate decision, as interns, who were on call twenty-four hours a day, weren't supposed to have wives, much less pregnant wives.

Where should they settle? New York was out of the question; Tom had two successful brothers there—Charlie, a lawyer, and Lloyd, an insurance broker—and he didn't want to live in their shadow. But staying in Baltimore would be worse; Edith would be there. Dr. Tom needed to be in charge of his world, and particularly of his wife, and he didn't plan to have his sister-in-law interfering with his influence.

Hartford, Connecticut, would be far enough away. Tom chose Hartford Hospital, though it was not his best offer. It catered to the poor, and the staff was not top-drawer; the older doctors scoffed at the "germ theory" and refused to wash their hands.

Still, it would give him a chance to do surgery, which he had decided to specialize in. This wasn't common at the time; the scalpel was merely one of the tools of the trade, like tongue depressors, and operating on patients was counted as simply part of the day's work. It suited Dr. Tom, though. He had no interest in the patient as a person with a problem. It was the mechanical aspects of surgery, later urinary surgery, that fascinated him, and he tackled them with dramatic flair, making a performance out of it, according to his colleagues.

Interns were strictly required to live in the hospital, but Tom and Kit secretly rented part of a house across the street. They rigged the bedroom up with a bell connected to the interns' quarters so he could sprint over to his duties at a moment's notice. Here, on November 8, 1905, little Tommy was born. He looked like Kit. His grandmother Nina transferred her ambitions to the baby. He would restore the family's glory.

They had no social life. Dr. Tom was always at the hospital and Kit was far from her family. She spent her days with the baby, gazing out the window at the busy world.

Edith and her husband came back from Germany, where Edith had been a caseworker with streetwalkers in Berlin, and lost no time opening a home for unwed mothers. Kit took care of baby Tommy and waited for the next one.

No birth certificate of Tom and Kit's eldest daughter survives. It's odd that a woman so famous should have a birth date so cloudy. For years it was given as November 8, 1909, but this was plainly wrong, as Tommy was always said to be two years older and he was born in 1905. Most sources have amended the date to November 8, 1907. Both the *Encyclopedia Britannica* and the meticulous biographer Barbara Leaming, however, give May 12, 1907, as her birth date.

Many actresses have maneuvered their birth dates by years, but a confusion of months and days remains an enigma. Perhaps neither date is correct. A psychologist might make something of the fact that November 8 was her adored brother Tommy's birthday and May 12 was her adored father's. (After he had known Kate for decades, playwright and director Garson Kanin, trying to find out when to send her a birthday card, sneaked a look at her passport, where he found a May date. When he confronted her with it, she laughed, claiming she had used her father's birthday for passport purposes.) When she was past eighty, photographer John Bryson, putting together a book about her, tried to pin her down on it, but she dodged airily, "Just use any of them."

In any case, at some point in 1907 Katharine Houghton Hepburn was born, with red hair like her father's.

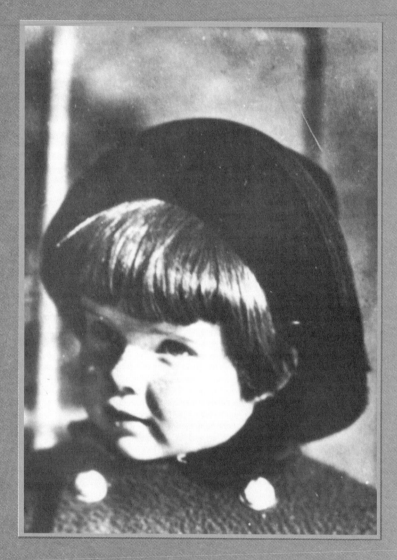

circa 1910

CHAPTER TWO

CHILDHOOD'S SUDDEN END

After the excitement and visitors that accompany a new baby had faded away, Kit was alone again, now with a baby and a toddler. Katharine Houghton Hepburn senior gazed at her son and at the red-haired daughter who was destined to fascinate millions for half a century, and she was bored. She loved her husband and children, but would there never be anything more?

It was Edith who rescued her and changed the direction of her life and her family's. Edith wrote her a passionate letter about her new crusade to change the sexual conduct of the country, to hold men as well as women up to moral standards. She was going to stamp out vice, close the brothels, get women the vote.

Hartford, it turned out, wasn't quite far enough from Edith after all. Young Mrs. Hepburn caught fire. She had found her calling.

Dr. Tom's surgery was going well. They moved to a comfortable house in the Nook Farm district, with trees and a stream. Carved over the fireplace were the words, LISTEN TO THE SONG OF LIFE. A cook, a maid, and a nanny were hired, leaving Mrs. Hepburn free to join the crusade. While Katharine was still a baby, Kit was elected president of the Connecticut Women's Suffrage Association.

From that day on, though she was to have four more children, Kit Hepburn was always busy in the world of women's rights, planning, directing, and organizing. Somehow she cajoled her husband into letting her roam, as long as she was back and sitting behind the tea table at precisely five o'clock when he came home.

Not surprisingly, she seems to have been a distant, though admired, figure in Katharine's childhood. Even when she was home, she never kissed or hugged or held her children. She did set aside bedtime for them and talked and read to them then. But it was Dr. Tom whom Katharine remembered most vividly, and apparently Dr. Tom who organized the children's lives.

The Hepburns believed, conveniently, in making the oldest child responsible for the safety and behavior of the younger ones. When Katharine took her first unsteady steps outdoors in the great world, it wasn't her mother who held her hand—it was her blond, serious-faced brother Tommy, two years older. When she was four she started kindergarten, and it was Tommy, not her mother, who walked her the complicated, mile-long journey to school.

When Dr. Tom came home at five, Mrs. Hepburn presided over tea, outdoors in the summertime, using tree stumps for chairs and tables. Then it was time for supervised athletics—baseball, prisoner's base, foot races, wrestling, and gymnastics. Katharine learned early to stand on her head, walk on her hands, and launch herself in flying somersaults from her father's shoulders. Sometimes Dr. Tom would look up from his tea and, in a voice that echoed through his children's lives as "the thunderous voice of God on high," would command Tommy to take off and run as fast as he could.

Tommy ran, but he could never run quite fast enough. Nothing he did was quite good enough for his father. By age four he had developed the nervous twitches of chorea, or Saint Vitus's dance. Dr. Tom knew, of course, that such tense, anxious children shouldn't be pushed to compete, but he could never admit of a problem in a child of his own. He told the boy sharply to control his twitches and run faster.

Mrs. Hepburn tried to assure the children that their father really loved them, that he just had trouble showing it. All the children were held to high standards of physical courage. When Katharine was three he put her on her first bike and, to teach her how to ride it, gave her a good hard push down a long steep hill. She survived. He urged them all to more and more reckless feats. He rigged a sixty-foot swinging ladder from the top of an elm tree and attached a trapeze and a rope that sloped perilously down to ground level along a gravel drive and into the back of the property. Little Kathy hung by her knees from the trapeze and rocketed through the woods to land with a thump. In winter, Dr. Tom attached a long rope to his car and the children fastened their sleds to it so he could careen them through the streets, speeding up, as the older Kate fondly remembered, around the corners to try to flip them off. Later he drilled them rigorously in diving. One stunt dive he insisted Kathy try knocked her out cold in the water.

Even granting that child-rearing customs of that time tended not to encourage the coddling of children, Dr. Tom's determination to make his offspring fearless seems so extreme as to be almost hostile. And his wife gave him a free rein, with Kathy as well as the boys. Of course Kit was much occupied with other matters, but also as a suffragist she must have read the work of the great suffragist Elizabeth Cady Stanton, who had written in 1851, "The girl must be allowed to romp and play, climb, skate, and swim; her clothing must be more like that of a boy . . . that she may be out at all times, and enter freely into all kinds of sport. . . . The manner in which all courage and self-reliance is educated out of the girl, her path portrayed with dangers and difficulties that never exist, is melancholy indeed." Just the same, it may have given Mrs. Hepburn a pang to see her small daughter rocketing past the second-story windows upside down on a trapeze.

When Kit was pregnant with her third child, Richard, she explained conception and birth to Kathy and Tommy. Kathy, age four, mulled this over and said, according to family tradition, "Then I can have a baby without getting married. That's what I shall do. I don't want any man bossing my children!" But in old age she would remember herself on the same occasion as having said she wouldn't marry "unless perhaps I can find a husband as nice as Dad."

Set the two versions side by side—one, the forthright reaction of a child with a domineering father; the other, the sanitized recollection of a woman desperate to remember her life as sunny, her childhood as rapturous, and her parents as perfect. For secret and pressing reasons, Katharine Hepburn kept editing her memory and revising her past. Dr. Tom's younger children recalled him as a ruthless, omnipotent bully; she clutched her own version of him as a loving deity presiding over the Eden that was her childhood.

"They brought us up with a feeling of freedom," she reminisces. "There were *no rules*." But elsewhere she says her father took considerable pride in being a spanking father: "Were we spanked? Beaten." If there were no rules to break, for what were the children beaten? For displeasing Dr. Tom, a stickler for instant obedience. A child who spoke out of turn would be publicly smacked across the face. Aunt Edith picked more than one quarrel with her brother-in-law for abusing his children.

Perhaps by "no rules" Kate meant that nobody cared where she went or what she did. At the age of four she was allowed to ride her bike alone all over Hartford. And always, when the children got sick, they were expected to keep quiet about it: "You were just supposed to stay out of sight until you felt better."

❖ ❖ ❖

"You're my favorite girl . . ."

In 1912, when Kathy was five, the Hepburns, with Aunt Edith and her husband, Don, bought a big shingled house at Fenwick on Long Island Sound and began spending summers there together. The house was built on a sandbar and had no plumbing or electricity, but everyone remembers the early summers there as idyllic. Kathy and Tom were, as always, inseparable, and the presence of wild water multiplied Dr. Tom's opportunities to train his children in fearlessness. The presence of Aunt Edith, now head of the Just Government League and editor of *Maryland Suffrage News*, multiplied the friction between him and her over the way to treat children.

During the winters in Hartford, Kathy was teased and picked on for her mother's very public activities and developed a chip on her shoulder. When she was a freckle-covered

THE HOUSE OF FENWICK

THE FIRST FENWICK, THE HEPBURN'S SUMMER RETREAT.

The sprawling Fenwick summer house was a wonderful place for a fearless child, free to explore in the wind and waves and fog. When Kathy was six she discovered a fishing shed on the beach and hung around the fishermen all day learning how to catch and fillet and cook a fish and how to manage a boat in rough weather.

She had a boat, of the type called a "sneakbox," considered highly unsafe at the best of times. Its name was *Tiger*. Anxious to show off her skills, Kathy coaxed Tommy out with her one stormy day. The waves were too much even for both of them. Swept three miles down the coast toward the open sea, the children were rescued just in time by some fishermen, but the *Tiger* was lost at sea, luckily with no hands on board.

Summer after summer the Hepburns and Edith and Don and all the young cousins returned to Fenwick. The other summer residents, rather a stuffy lot, representing the conservative executives of Hartford's main industry, Aetna Life Insurance, were deeply shocked by the radical Mrs. Hepburn and her involvement in unladylike causes. Their children came to the Hepburns' to play, though, bribed by food and freedom from rules.

There were tennis courts and a primitive nine-hole golf course, and diving contests and three-legged races and sailboat races. To those whose idea of a summer retreat is a sandy beach towel and a stack of murder mysteries, Fenwick sounds exhausting. The young Hepburns, urged on by their father, competed fiercely to run the fastest, sail closest to the wind, swim out the farthest, dive the highest, brave the most dangers, and beat all comers at golf and tennis.

At Fenwick, when Kathy was in her early teens, she and a friend, Alice Barbour, took up a secret life of crime and crept out at night to break into neighboring houses, climbing over roofs and dropping down skylights, purely for the sport of it. By daylight, she and Alice produced a play, *Beauty and the Beast*—Kathy was the Beast—for which they sold tickets and raised seventy-five dollars to send to the Navajo Indians.

Fenwick remained the anchor of the grown-up Kate's world, and she retreated there whenever she could. Then came the hurricane of 1938. Kate was there with her mother, her brother Dick, Fanny the cook, and a guest. After her morning swim, she noticed with interest that a car, some boats, and chunks of houses were flying past the windows. Mrs. Hepburn, convinced the house would stand, refused to leave until Dick dragged her out through the dining-room window into deep water. The others followed, and they groped their way to higher ground.

When Kate came back the next day there was nothing left but a toilet and a bathtub. She and Dick dug in the sand searching for her mother's silverware. They found eighty-five pieces, and also the sacred tea service, but nothing more.

Kate gave her father money to rebuild. Where their beloved, ramshackle cottage had stood he built a steel-enforced brick showplace, designed to be grander than all the neighbors' houses and show them Dr. Hepburn was doing well.

Still, land and wind and water remained, and Kate in her old age withdrew there happily, still swimming all winter in Long Island Sound.

nine-year-old she cut off her hair, called herself Jimmy, and took to wearing Tommy's clothes to school, where she got in fights. She snatched cookies at her mother's political meetings and waved flags in her mother's parades, defying hecklers and enjoying the attention. With World War I, public opinion had turned against the women's movement as unpatriotic. Mrs. Hepburn's house was headquarters for radical women like Emmeline Pankhurst, Margaret Sanger, and Rebecca West, and sometimes people threw rocks through the windows. Many respectable Hartford families wouldn't allow their children to play with the Hepburns.

In the spring of 1915, Kathy's uncle Charles, Dr. Tom's older brother and a respectable New York lawyer, dressed for work one morning and then jumped out the window, impaling himself on an iron picket fence four flights below. Though it made headlines, the family insisted, then and forever, that he had simply been looking out the window and lost his balance.

It was the first suicide for the Hepburns, the third in Kathy's immediate family.

The Hepburns moved to a new house in Hartford, and Dr. Tom built a gymnasium in it to keep his children in tough, competitive shape. Kathy worked tirelessly to win his approval. Tommy, as a boy and the eldest, could never be quite good enough to win it, though he excelled at track, swimming, wrestling, tennis, and golf. At the Kingswood School he starred in football, basketball, baseball, and track. He was constantly training but, like his father, was never satisfied. He seemed nervous and had nightmares.

When she was twelve, Kathy started at the Oxford School, sister school to Tommy's. She was weak in Latin but at least she had stopped dressing in Tommy's clothes. She played a forget-me-not in *The Dance of the Flowers* and was tops in fig-

Katharine Hepburn (left) with her sisters Margaret (center) and Marion (right).

ure skating, tennis, and golf, though only number two in the high jump, no matter how hard she practiced.

The Nineteenth Amendment, granting votes for women, was ratified on August 26, 1920. This marked a major victory for the suffragists, though Mrs. Hepburn considered it only the first step in the fight for equality. Shortly afterward, a committee of prominent Democrats approached her and asked her to run for the United States Senate. Having given birth to Robert, Marion, and Margaret, she had now produced the six children Dr. Tom considered essential for people of their desirable genetic heritage. And now she wanted something for herself. She wanted to run for the Senate.

When she told Dr. Tom she'd been asked to, he said, "Well, fine, Kit, when do we get our divorce?"

And that was the end of that.

In the spring of 1921, Tommy, now a tall, good-looking, broad-shouldered fifteen, was showing signs of strain so obvious that even the Hepburns, determined to have perfect children, were forced to notice. A special treat was arranged for his distraction—a five-day trip with Kathy to New York to visit his godmother, Mary Towle, whom the Hepburn children called Aunty.

Tommy took full responsibility for his thirteen-year-old sister on the journey, buying return trip tickets before they left the station in New York, and they arrived promptly at Towle's little house in Greenwich Village, where they'd often been before. Tommy was in tearing high spirits and said it was the happiest experience of his life. He was to sleep on a cot in the third-floor attic storeroom full of old furniture; Kathy, downstairs.

On Friday night, the three of them went merrily uptown to a movie, a silent comedy based on Mark Twain's *A Connecticut Yankee in King Arthur's Court.* Comedy it may have been, but there was a brief scene of a hanging in it that affected Tommy violently. He told Kathy in private that it had given him the horrors, and he was struggling to control himself.

She must have remembered that only a year before, she and Dr. Tom had found Tommy trying out a stunt with a noose, pretending to hang himself. At the time, Tommy insisted he was only re-creating a trick his father had often talked about from his wild youth, when he and his friends staged a mock lynching to scandalize a visiting football team, using a black man who could tense his neck muscles so that he wouldn't choke. Dr. Tom, apparently undaunted by the suicides already in the family, told his son not to do it again.

After the movie, Tommy wrestled with the horrors all through the next day's sightseeing, and by Saturday evening he seemed to be in control again. He played his banjo for Aunty and Kathy, and said, "You're my favorite girl in the whole world." (At least, she thinks he did. Later she wasn't sure. Maybe she made it up. Or dreamed it.) At ten o'clock they all went to bed.

Tommy didn't come down to breakfast Sunday morning. Kathy and Aunty ate alone, but there was a train to be caught, and at nine Kathy climbed the stairs to the attic and banged on the door, calling "Sleepyhead!" Silence. She rattled the door. It was locked. Frightened, she forced it open.

Tommy was dead. The dearly loved brother who had been her companion all her life, who had held her hand when she took her first steps, was hanging from a rafter, his skin bluish-purple.

Apparently Tommy had miscalculated at first—the rope he'd made out of torn strips of bed sheet was too long. He had tied it to a metal bedspring on the floor and thrown the end over a rafter, slipped the noose over his head, and jumped from a crate—and landed on his feet. He reached over and hauled on the bedspring to tighten the noose, and with fierce single-mindedness managed to strangle himself. It couldn't have been easy.

The phone calls were made. The police came. At the morgue the assistant medical examiner put it down as "asphyxia by hanging (suicide)." It was the fourth suicide.

When Dr. and Mrs. Hepburn got to the city, Kathy had already answered the questions of the police and the crowd that had gathered. Dr. Tom shooed them away and firmly denied that it could have been suicide. Not his son. He told the police someone must have broken into the house and strangled him, then tried to cover up the murder.

The police found no evidence of an intruder.

Dr. Tom assured reporters that Tommy was healthy and athletic and ambitious and didn't have a care in the world. Later he changed his story and said it must have been a sudden impulse, a fit of adolescent insanity. Later still he said it was just a childish stunt that went wrong. Never, never must it look as if a demanding father drove a nervous boy into a fit of calamitous depression.

It's possible Tommy had been struggling secretly with "the horrors" for all his fifteen years. He could hardly have told his family of such a shameful weakness.

In Annapolis, depressed by the news, still another of Kathy's uncles, Dr. Sewell Hepburn, sealed himself in his garage and turned the car's engine on and sat in the driver's seat until he died. It was reported that he had suffered a heart attack while working on his car.

That made five.

Within the Hepburn family, silence fell like a curtain over the death of its brightest hope. Tommy's ashes, in a candy box, were dropped hastily into a grave that was never to be visited. The memory of Tommy was excised from the family dialogue. As Kate later proudly remembered, her parents "simply did not believe in moaning about anything."

The mother was never allowed to mourn her eldest and probably favorite child. Edith, her lifelong confidant, blamed Dr. Tom and broke off with the family, leaving Kit alone with her silence. And Kathy, the sister who had adored him, was left alone to come to terms with her brother's death and to keep silent, to protect Dr. Tom from what he refused to know.

Probably she was wrenched in all directions with guilt: Who else could and should have saved him but the sister he'd confided in, the one who knew him best?

Encased in the silence, Katharine's memory blurred and rearranged itself until she was no longer sure of the facts and felt she'd dreamed some of them, such as rushing across the street to a doctor's house, where a woman who opened the door said that if Tommy was dead, then the doctor couldn't help him, and slammed the door.

In her memoirs Katharine Hepburn briefly turns the laser beam of her relentlessly joyful hindsight on this festering sore, as if to shrivel it to nothing, and then hurries on with face averted. Perhaps her urgent need to be happy sprang from an endless struggle against the family's double strand of depression.

Perhaps she was always running from it, looking over her shoulder, always running from her brother's self-destruction.

Katharine Hepburn at age 14.

CHAPTER THREE

OUT IN THE WORLD

N o one—probably least of all herself—could know what was happening inside young Kathy in the years after Tommy's death. Her parents, though they may have worried secretly, didn't inquire. Her mother's only theory of grief therapy was to keep busy. Edith, with more insight into troubling matters, might have helped, but she had turned her back in anger on the Hepburns, and after nine summers at Fenwick, she and her family came no more. Don Hooker sold his share in the house to Dr. Tom, and they summered in Maine instead.

Kathy at first threw herself into schoolwork in an effort to avoid conversation. Before, she had played with her brothers and sisters; now she aligned herself with the grown-ups as a kind of third parent. At school she was withdrawn and suspicious, dodging her friends. At Fenwick, she attacked her golf and diving furiously, as if trying to exhaust herself into oblivion or trying to excel at everything to make up for the loss of Dr. Tom's eldest son. Trying to replace Tommy, perhaps even turn into Tommy, may have been the only way for Kathy to accept his death.

She had always had vague dreams of being an actress, but now with Tommy gone she decided to study medicine as he had been expected to do. Though she still put on shows for her little brothers, with cardboard actors in a wooden box, at the end of that summer she didn't go back to the Oxford School but was tutored instead, with an eye on Bryn Mawr. This intensified her isolation from friends and her dependence on her parents for company and approval. On Saturday nights she went with her father to the movies.

Mrs. Hepburn didn't go to movies. She thought they were silly. After a stretch of her own silent, isolated withdrawal, she was back in the women's movement, tackling the restrictive birth-control laws. In Connecticut then it was illegal to use, prescribe, or even mention any kind of birth control at all, and Mrs. Hepburn laid about with a cudgel, even traveling to Washington to beard Congress in its den; the congressmen, embarrassed at the very words, giggled and nudged each other.

Kathy, unlicensed and underage, was allowed to borrow her mother's car to drive to her tutoring sessions and her daily lessons with the pro at the Hartford Golf Club. Anxious and nervous, she took the Bryn Mawr entrance exam, but unlike her mother, she passed the first time around, and with flying colors. In the fall of 1924 she moved into Pembroke West, the same building in which her mother and aunt had presided over some infamous dinner parties.

Kathy wasn't happy. She had been away from school for four years and had forgotten how to socialize. Away from her family for the first time, she was paralyzed with shyness and suspicion. She stayed as much as possible in her rooms and took her cold shower at four in the morning to avoid running into her neighbors. She even ate her meals alone, sometimes scraps Ali Barbour brought her from the dining hall. Ali, her old friend and fellow burglar from Fenwick days, started as a classmate but dropped out after her freshman year to get married.

Kathy, now called Kate, shrank even from her beloved athletics, pretending to be terrible at them. She was a puzzle to such other girls as noticed her at all. As she recalls, her entire wardrobe consisted of a blue skirt and an Icelandic sweater that she wore every day, no doubt in tribute to her father's wardrobe philosophy; as part of his spartan creed, Dr. Tom never owned more than two suits and one pair of shoes at a time. It seems likely that Kate had more, and better, clothes. However preoccupied she may have been, Mrs. Hepburn gave considerable thought to her own wardrobe, careful always to look feminine and respectable to her audience when she delivered her fiery speeches. It's hard to imagine that she sent her pretty daughter off to college with only two garments, yet Kate's classmates remember her clothes as peculiar, to say the least. Perhaps her mother had packed clothes for her that she ignored.

Huddled in her rooms alone, Kate might have been studying, but evidently she wasn't. Her grades were a disgrace. She did so badly in chemistry that it was plain she wouldn't replace Tommy in the next generation of doctors. She switched her major to history, and later again to English.

After an emergency appendectomy that her father insisted on performing himself, she was late starting her sophomore year, still bewildered and drifting. All the manic energy that had fueled her days since Tommy's death had leaked away into some dark corner of her mind. The only three girls she had known before arriving at Bryn Mawr had all dropped out. Her grades kept slipping. In the spring the administration advised Dr. Tom to withdraw her, but he couldn't admit defeat for a child of his. He sent her back, over her protests that she wanted to quit and become an actress.

She may have had a very close call. In later years her memory of the time stumbled badly, as if this blurred, dark time didn't bear remembering. Searching through her memoirs and interviews, it's impossible to pin down whether something happened then, or years earlier, or years before. It's almost as if, in her effort to obliterate that morning she found Tommy, she damaged the interior clockwork that records a person's life.

In those first years at Bryn Mawr she may have slid perilously close to becoming another secret family statistic, but the women of the Houghton-Hepburn clan were made of stronger fiber than the men. She shook off the despair, with help from a new friend, the brilliant and outgoing Alice Palache. Kate began to study. She spent as much time in the library as she had previously spent alone in her rooms. Once, after working there all night, she refreshed herself by taking off all her clothes and bathing in the M. Carey Thomas memorial fountain.

Stripping was never an obstacle to Kate, whose parents habitually strolled naked around the house, even when they had guests; biographer Barbara Leaming suggests that nudity chez Hepburn was part of their mask of utter openness and honesty, along with shocking dinner guests by discussing syphilis, or the mechanics of conception, or the problems of the urinary tract. Dr. and Mrs. Hepburn were always totally frank about everything—except for the things that really mattered.

Kate's dip in the fountain made her famous, and she became a part of campus life. Thanks to Palache, she pulled up her grades and was now eligible for dramatics. She chopped off her hair and played Oliver, the leading man in *The Truth About Blayds*, in white pants and a blazer and tie. The play ran for two nights on campus in April 1927 and then did a benefit performance at the Colony Club in New York.

That summer Kate went to Europe with Palache, and they had a wonderful time, living on tomato sandwiches and chocolates and washing in the rest rooms of pubs. They bought a cheap car and drove all over England, Scotland, and Wales, then sold the car back to its previous owner and sailed home penniless but happy. Kate had fought her way out of a dark patch of woods.

She recovered her spirits almost too well. Bryn Mawr suspended her for five days for smoking. She became something of a daredevil hero to her classmates, posing naked on a roof in a blizzard, climbing down drainpipes and vines after hours, joyriding in a friend's car late at night, and throwing herself into sports and dramatics. When she appeared in a play called *The Cradle Song*, a bewildered student reviewer said she was so wonderful to look at that it was hard to pass judgment on her acting—a dilemma that was to plague other reviewers for years.

In the spring of her senior year Kate was chosen to play Pandora, the lead in *The Woman in the Moon*, a sixteenth-century comedy never before produced in America. It was at this pinnacle of her college life that she met Jack Clarke, a social register type with a house near the campus, and his best friend, Ludlow Ogden Smith, called "Luddy," a well-heeled young man from a Main Line Philadelphia family.

Kate admired Luddy. He had fought in World War I and studied at the University of Grenoble. With enough money to be carefree, he dabbled in music, art, and photography. When Kate obligingly posed nude for him at his country retreat, the

THE PATIENT, FAITHFUL LUDDY

In the 1990s, Luddy would have been offered a multimillion-dollar advance and a ghostwriter to write the book of his lifelong relationship with Kate, and we would have known more about him, perhaps more than we needed to know. As it is, he's hard to understand.

Kate's biographer Anne Edwards, musing on the marriage, says, "He did not seem to be head over heels in love with her either," though they were "wonderfully good friends." She hints darkly at a possible Oedipal relationship with his mother and says he was "coming to terms . . . with his own sexuality." Perhaps, she suggests, Kate thought of him as a replacement for her lost brother and hoped to do a better job of rescuing him. She mentions rumors that their marriage was platonic.

Others disagree. Leaming says he couldn't keep his hands off her, and that his intense physical attraction to her was more obvious than ever after they were married. She believes that Kate returned the passion and thoroughly enjoyed sex, her parents having always praised the "complete satisfaction of sexual desire" so essential to marriage.

In her own book, *Me*, Kate calls her only husband and friend of over half a century "an odd-looking man," but adds that he was "the soul of sensitivity." Hardly the words of a passionate lover, but then Katharine Hepburn was the soul of reticence. Nearing thirty, Ludlow Ogden Smith seems to have been at loose ends when Kate, age twenty, flashed into his life to pose nude in his living room. Reportedly tall and broad-shouldered, he oiled his hair and combed it back after the fashion of the times. He spoke several languages and, with his Main Line background and his Grenoble education, struck Kate as sophisticated. His friends all describe him as sensitive and rather sad, but he could also raise a giggle by touching his nose with the tip of his tongue. Unlike Dr. Tom, he never took himself quite seriously and could even laugh at his own passion for Kate. With sufficient money and no pressing career, he was ready to fall in love. For a gentle fellow from a prim, repressed family, the uninhibited Kate was a natural target.

On his first visit to Fenwick,

Luddy was stumbling around a dark hallway when the lights went on and he suddenly beheld his future father-in-law wearing nothing but a very brief shirt, his nether anatomy casually exposed. Apparently he was charmed. The family was charmed, too, and took to Luddy so strongly that Mrs. Hepburn even forgave him for voting for Herbert Hoover and tried to convert him to socialism. All the Hepburns felt he was too sweet, too eager to please, to stand up to their bossy Kate, and they tried to protect him from her.

To add to his qualifications, Luddy was handy around the house; the Hepburns took pride in being hopeless at fixing things, and everything at Fenwick tended to break, from furnace to toaster. Luddy coped with the unreliable plumbing and wiring; when anything went wrong, the family just waited for his next visit. They didn't even mind that he was rather a bore at the dinner table. The Hepburns hadn't approved of any of Kate's other gentlemen callers, and their wholehearted acceptance of this one must have gone far to raise him in her esteem.

Even after their divorce, Luddy continued to be a member of the family, accepted as one of their own and visiting regularly at Fenwick without waiting for an invitation; he simply showed up with his ever-present camera and, presumably, a screwdriver. When Kate brought a new suitor to meet her family, Luddy would be there as one of them, following Kate and her beau around snapping pictures of them, still a tireless nuisance of a photographer.

There are no anecdotes about Luddy. He had no adventures to relate, no close calls in an open boat, no daredevil accidents or even smashing tennis victories. His talent was patience. Kate's men might come and go, but Luddy would always be there waiting. When he was in his seventies, after he had remarried and then been widowed, he would visit Kate at Fenwick, and she would welcome him and cook dinner for him. After dinner he would tinker with the balky furnace or fix a leaky faucet. When he fell ill, she brought him his meals until he died, in 1979. He had outwaited them all.

path of Luddy's life took a sharp turn from which it never quite recovered.

The Woman in the Moon was produced for the big May Day celebration, with a long winter finally over and every flower on the campus in bloom. The Hepburns were there. Luddy was there. So was a then-famous poet named E. Phelps Putnam, who was instantly smitten. Kate, barefoot in a flowing gown, looks dazzling in a surviving photograph of the production; in person she must have been astounding. She played the part as a romping tomboy rather than a delicate maiden, and though her father said all he could see was her dirty feet getting dirtier and her face getting redder, others disagreed.

Jack Clarke gave Kate a letter of introduction to a producer in Baltimore with a stock company. After final exams, she slipped off to Baltimore and badgered her way into a part as a lady-in-waiting in his upcoming production of *The Czarina*. That much was easy. The hard part was telling her father.

After graduating from Bryn Mawr with honors, Kate drove her parents home to West Hartford. In the car, she broke the news of her career choice. Dr. Tom, predictably, exploded with rage. He demanded that she stop the car and let him out; he would take a train. He said acting was silly, actors were egomaniacs, and the whole enterprise was nothing but vanity.

The battle raged on while she prepared to leave for Baltimore. When she left the house with her suitcase, he shouted after her, "You just want to show off and get paid for it!" Looking back in her old age, she cheerfully admitted that he was right.

For a young woman who had spent the first twenty years of her life trying to please her father, it was a remarkable leap into her own life, but it must have been jarring. Toward the end of her life she still remembered that he "thought acting was a silly profession, closely allied to streetwalking," and that she "had developed into a cheap show-off." He was not going to change his mind after she got famous, either. He was not a flexible man. In later years, when asked if he was Katharine Hepburn's father, he always replied indignantly that, no, she was Thomas Hepburn's daughter. And she was. The stubborn will that drove him drove her, too, and gave her the strength to defy him.

∾ ∾ ∾

"... *personality and charm*"

She barged into the Baltimore stock company wearing dirty sneakers, baggy pants, and an ancient sweater, and she strode around the stage as if on a golf course; but the other members of the company took a fancy to her and gave her a hand. The actor Kenneth MacKenna tried to slow down her delivery and keep her from getting so intense. After the two-week engagement, he sent her to a voice coach in New York, Frances Robinson-Duff, with a note saying she had "talent and loads of personality and charm," but "stands awfully and never sits in a chair if there's an inch of floor available."

So young Katharine Hepburn was off to New York, the one place everyone wanted to be in the giddy years of the late '20s, the sparkling fountainhead of art and theater and literature, of wit and wildness and the Algonquin Round Table. Her parents forgave her; her father even apologized, grudgingly, and sent her the money for Robinson-Duff's coaching. Phelps Putnam, the poet who had been so struck by her as Pandora at Bryn Mawr, found her immediately and gathered her into his curiously chaste bed.

Though Putnam is forgotten now, even in poetical circles, in 1928 he was considered one of the country's most promising poets. The year before, his first book of poems, *Trinc*, had been praised by major critics as the work of a powerful new voice. He was compared to F. Scott Fitzgerald and Ernest Hemingway. He was thirty-four, handsome, dark, hard-drinking, moody, and, like most of Kate's subsequent men, married. He and his wife lived in Boston. He and Kate frolicked in a friend's apartment on East 54th Street. He wrote reams of poetry about her and the beauty of her naked body and her vitality, which he claimed had cured his writer's block. He introduced her to the people who mattered in New York, the crowd around Robert Benchley and Dorothy Parker and Edmund Wilson, and he took her to all the places where the great artistic revolution was happening. The New Yorkers were charmed by Kate's oddness, even by her frequent trips to the bathroom (because, as she told them, her father had told her always to drink great quantities of water all day). She was accepted as something new, an "original."

What Putnam didn't do was actually consummate the relationship, for all Kate's blandishments. She was wild about him, but he claimed his passion was so intense as to be far beyond mere sex. Presently he left her and went off to write in Nova Scotia.

Abandoned, Kate took up with Luddy Smith again. He was living in New York now and so obviously in love with her that, in a friend's empty apartment, she lost the virginity she'd offered to Putnam. As she later recalled, "there didn't seem to be any reason not to." She had been in love with Putnam, but Luddy was a friend, and a friend he would always remain.

Kate's first New York performance was not in Manhattan but in the Great Neck Theater on Long Island. She was originally hired to understudy the leading lady in what was to be a single pre-Broadway performance of *The Big Pond*, but the leading lady was fired. Here, just as in the stories, was Kate's big break, after only a few weeks in New York.

Many in the sophisticated audience recognized Kate from her travels with Putnam and gave her entrance an enthusiastic hand. It made her giddy with excitement; she was a star! Wired up with the joy of it, she dashed madly around the stage and gabbled her lines so manically that no one could understand a word she said. The next day she was fired.

A producer named Arthur Hopkins had been in the audience, however, and in spite of her clumsy, keyed-up performance, he sensed the energy of her personality and called her into his office. She promptly accepted his offer of a small part as a schoolgirl in his new play *These Days*, set to try out in New Haven and Hartford before opening on Broadway.

In the meantime she was suddenly famous, or notorious, as the heroine with the fox-colored hair in Phelps Putnam's impassioned new poem, "Daughters of the Sun." He was back from Nova Scotia, bubbling with satisfaction, and giving recitations of it everywhere. No one in the know doubted who its sexy subject was. Now Kate was torn between her romantic passion for Putnam and her affection for Luddy, who, as he always would, waited patiently. Finally, wrenched with ambivalence, Putnam withdrew from the fray and faded into obscurity. "Daughters of the Sun," soaring on the wings of Kate's energy, had been his fifteen minutes of fame.

These Days played New Haven and Hartford and moved on to the Cort Theater in New York. The only bits of the reviews Kate read were the ones that noticed and praised her, so she was startled to learn that the play itself had been so severely panned it was closing Saturday.

Her next job was a comedown: understudying Hope

Williams in the Philip Barry play *Holiday*. The play was a hit, and Hope Williams, the star, immensely popular—an aristocratic, sophisticated New Yorker with a distinctive swagger. The general feeling was that the gangly hoyden Kate would make a dim substitute. Just the same, Kate went to the theater every night and sat and waited, in case Williams might be struck by lightning in the second act. Every evening she asked Williams, "How are you feeling tonight?" Every evening, Williams felt fine. All Kate's bounding energy sat harnessed to a chair, night after night. It can't have been comfortable, and though she doesn't admit it in her memoirs, she was never one to take it kindly when other women were applauded and praised.

After two weeks she quit the job and married Luddy.

It still comes as a shock to Katharine Hepburn fans that she actually married anyone at all, given her many statements that marriage was an unnatural arrangement, and that men and women were not really suited to live together. More surprising still, why marry this amiable but unexciting man, by no means her equal? Of course, though she would never admit it of her perfect parents' perfect marriage, Kate had had many years to watch her strong-minded mother knuckle under to her even more strong-minded father. A wimp might not seem such a bad idea.

Apparently, at least for the moment, Kate fully expected to become a wife to Luddy, just as her mother before her had put aside her restless youth to settle down as the doctor's wife. Kate herself, in her memoirs, said she did it because she had the perfect dress to wear, crushed white velvet with gold embroidery. Dress or no dress, the decision remains something of a mystery no one, perhaps least of all Kate, could understand. Mrs. Hepburn said, "If you want to sacrifice the admiration of many men for the criticism of one, go ahead, get married." She spoke from hard experience, but she was wrong; other men still admired, and Luddy never criticized.

Kate's grandfather, Parson Hep, married them under extremely private circumstances on December 12, 1928. Because Kate balked at being known as "Mrs. Smith," the obliging Luddy renamed himself Ogden Ludlow. Kate, however, failed to take advantage of his sacrifice and never used her new last name. They spent a brief honeymoon in Bermuda and then went to look at real estate near Luddy's family home, "Sherraden," in Strafford on Philadelphia's Main Line.

Katharine Hepburn senior's embrace of domesticity lasted two years. Katharine junior's lasted two weeks.

circa 1934

CHAPTER FOUR

UPS AND DOWNS

Katharine Hepburn senior, on the streets of Hartford pushing a baby carriage and leading a toddler, suddenly stopped and wondered if this was all her life would offer. Katharine junior, a bride of two weeks, went to look at houses on the Main Line and said to herself, "What am I doing? I can't live here."

Perhaps Luddy had looked forward to returning to the settled, orderly, restrictive life of a suburban Philadelphian in the social register, but he made no objection when Kate whisked them back to New York and into a brownstone on East 39th Street. She went straight to Arthur Hopkins to get her old understudy job back. "Yes, of course," he said. "I expected you."

It was an odd life the newlyweds led. Luddy would come home from his job as an insurance broker in time to watch Kate dash off on foot across town to the theater. In the evenings he fiddled with his model train set, of which he was uncommonly fond, listened to Wagner's operas, and waited for his dinner to be sent in.

At the theater, few people even knew Kate was married. She waited for Hope Williams to get sick, but winter passed, spring came, and though once she came down with flu and practically had to be carried on stage, Williams played every show. When *Holiday* closed its Broadway run in the spring, Kate had spent six months waiting in vain to play the lead. (In the fall, when the show was getting ready to go on tour, she did play the Williams part once, wearing clothes too small for her, and by her own admission was pretty bad. The Williams debutante air defied imitation.)

Kate had no agent, though she says she did once or twice go sit forlornly all day in agents' offices, always dressed in her bag-lady clothes to show that she didn't give a damn. After she was famous, her clothes grew famous, too; wherever she went she wore her signature turtlenecks and baggy pants. (Once, visiting Spencer Tracy at the dignified Claridge's in London, she was told that, movie star or no movie star, she'd have to use the trades-men's entrance and stop shocking the lobby with her trousers. Heading to Africa to make *The African Queen*, she observed with satisfaction that she didn't have to buy a new wardrobe for the jungle, as her usual clothes were far more suited to Africa than to the places in which they were usually seen.) But at least later her trademark casual clothes were all in one piece. At college, like her aunt Edith before her, and in her early years scrounging for parts in plays, she seems to have been wearing rags. People remember her clothes as being held together with safety pins. Where did a young woman of such respectable background even find such garments? And why? Her mother was always impecca-bly dressed; was this a rebellion against her, maybe even a touch of secret hostility? Or was Kate simply looking for attention or trying not to seem anxious to please?

She had a letter of introduction to the Theater Guild, which led to a reading for the ingenue part in *Meteor*. She won the part, but then something better came along—the lead in *Death Takes a Holiday*—and she turned down the first offer. When *Death* opened in its tryout tour in Washington, D.C., one reviewer observed cattily that Kate looked "like a death's head with a metallic voice." The show went on to Philadelphia, where she was fired. Her parents drove down to catch her last performance and thought she was awful; "galumphing there like a maniac," her father said. Next she understudied the ingenue in Turgenev's *A Month in the Country*, but the star took a dislike to her and got her fired. Then Kate went off to play in summer stock at the Berkshire Playhouse with her new friend, the heiress Laura Harding. That lasted two weeks. She didn't like the roles she was offered and managed to irritate everyone before flouncing off in a huff.

Kate was flailing. Her mother had always told her that the world was run by the strong and that it was dangerous to be weak, but Kit Hepburn's strength lay in getting her own way by tact and indirection. She had learned in a hard school. Kate, however, had no use for tact. The egocentric will she'd inherited from Dr. Tom couldn't be bent to subtlety. When she felt that others were in charge of her life she turned thorny and defiant. Many people who knew her at the time remembered her as an irritant.

The popular playwright Philip Barry, however, was inspired by the very qualities that annoyed others. He was writing a play for her, *The Animal Kingdom*, about a man torn between wife and mistress, with echoes of Kate's well-known affair with the poet Phelps Putnam. The role of Daisy was Kate's, and it was a wonderful role. Barry persuaded the producer, Gilbert Miller, that she was the only possible choice, and Miller, against his better judgment, agreed. Here it was, the big break, the turning point, the moment of Kate's triumphant arrival on Broadway.

The play went into rehearsal in the fall of 1931. Five days into rehearsals, Leslie Howard, the leading man, said he couldn't work with Kate and had her fired.

Kate and Barry, whom she was later to owe so much, had a shouting match, with Kate in a blazing fury and Barry retorting, "Nobody with your vicious disposition could possibly play light comedy!" The big break had collapsed before it began.

A woman of a different temperament might have retired to the Main Line with Luddy and become famous for her rose gardens and tea parties, but not Dr. Tom and Kit Hepburn's daughter. In the spring of 1932 producer Harry Moses was mounting a new play, *The Warrior's Husband.* Hope Williams had committed to play the lead, the Amazon warrior Antiope, but she changed her mind and opted for something more artistic. Moses then offered the part to the woman who had understudied Williams for so long in *Holiday.*

Any actor would have given his or her left foot to make the entrance Kate made as Antiope. Her arms and legs bronzed with makeup, in a scrap of a metallic tunic and silver shin guards, she enters leaping down a high narrow stairway at the back of the stage with a dead stag slung over her shoulder. She strides across the stage, slams the stag down before the Queen of the Amazons, drops to one knee, and bellows, "Get me a bowl of water, will you? I'm in a terrific sweat!"

Screen tests followed promptly, and in July, after the play had closed, Katharine Hepburn was on her way to Hollywood, RKO contract in hand.

She traveled on the *Super Chief* with Laura Harding (who was giving her an excellent education in how the rich behaved) and Laura's two terriers. It must have been a merry journey, until the point when Kate pried open a train window for a breath of air and instead got an eyeful of tiny steel splinters. She arrived in Pasadena on a sweltering day in July 1932, howling for a doctor. Leland Hayward, her agent, tried to ignore her howling, introduce her around, and show her the studio. No one believed she had something in her eye; in fact, its crimsoned condition gave rise to an immediate rumor that she drank. Director George Cukor tried to interest her in hair-styles and costumes, but she was in considerable pain and couldn't pay attention. Her hair had already been cut short, and the day was over before she was finally taken to a woman doctor in her office in downtown Los Angeles, who removed the splinters. On her first morning on the job, Kate showed up with an eye patch and, according to writer Adela Rogers St. John, who was on the lot, her clothes were "the most appalling and incredible I have ever seen in my life. They looked like something . . . for the Mexican army to go ski-jumping in." Not an auspicious beginning.

❧ ❧ ❧

"She is so real, so genuine . . ."

The great producer David O. (*Gone With the Wind*) Selznick found her sexually repellent. The word among the RKO brass was that she looked "like a cross between a horse and a monkey."

Kate was to play John Barrymore's daughter in *A Bill of Divorcement*, and happily the aging matinee idol, hard-drinking darling of women all over the world, took her under his wing.

As Sydney Fairfield in A Bill of Divorcement.

Naturally he made a pass at her—he was constitutionally unable to keep his hands off any woman in the immediate area—but when she simply stared at him in blank astonishment he desisted cheerfully. She played Sydney Fairfield, whose father has been shell-shocked in World War I and who gives up her own fiancé and future to care for him.

Kate and the movie camera were made for each other. Stage work, especially in the eyes of those beyond the fifth row, is largely a matter of voice and movement; Kate's voice grated on many people and her movements weren't always quite under her full control. The camera, however, loves faces, especially strong faces like Kate's, with its dramatic sweeping line from eye socket to nose; the unforgettable sculpted cheekbones; the rich, full mouth. On film, her movements took on an emotional significance they had lacked onstage. She was immediately at home in front of the camera, as relaxed as she had been posing nude for Luddy in college. Gone was the anxious tension that had sometimes pushed her stage performances over the edge into hysteria. And in the movies, as she said, "If you didn't get it right the first time, you could do it again. Besides, I always thought theater audiences were out to get me."

She went on making trouble, though. Following her usual custom, Kate dropped out for frequent baths and showers during the day. She came to work in disreputable blue jeans, hardly the custom at the time, which delighted the lurking news photographers and enraged the studio. RKO authorities threatened to steal her jeans and hide them from her. One day when she went to her dressing room they were gone. She announced that if she didn't get them back immediately, she would walk around in her underwear. The offending garment was not returned and, "Of course I did it," she recalled. "I walked through the lot in my underpants." The jeans speedily reappeared.

Selznick continued to think she was a disaster until the trade papers passed judgment on the early previews, late in August. They disagreed with him. The *Hollywood Reporter* called the movie a milestone and raved about the "new star on the cinema horizon," predicting that she would "capture followers by the millions." The *Hollywood Herald* gushed, "She is so real, so genuine—well, darn it all what's her next picture? We want a front seat!" Selznick swallowed his distaste and gave Kate a new contract. And Leland Hayward, equally impressed by the reviews, took a sudden interest in his rising new client.

While John Barrymore simply grabbed for the nearest woman, Hayward was choosier. He liked them famous. He was, as he himself bragged, a scalp-hunter, and if Katharine Hepburn was going to be famous, Hayward would be first in line.

When their affair began, Leland Hayward was married, for the second time, to Lola Gibbs. His conquests had included Clara Bow, Janet Gaynor, Marlene Dietrich, and Greta Garbo. Later he would marry the actress Margaret Sullavan at the peak of her fame and, some wives after that, Pamela Churchill (later Pamela Harriman, later U.S. ambassador to France). Pamela was always convinced that he'd loved Kate best of all, but Kate was dubious. They'd just had fun, she recalled.

Reasons can be found for Kate's marrying Luddy, but even her most resolute fans find it hard to accept her affair with Hayward. He couldn't possibly have reminded her of her brother or her father or anyone else she'd known. Though it can hardly have impressed the austere Kate, he was a snappy dresser with dazzling cuff links and three hundred pairs of shoes. Handsome in the bland classical manner of F. Scott Fitzgerald, he was a well-practiced charmer, easy company, and an accomplished talker. Looking back, in *Me*, Kate says, "And it wasn't long before we . . . Well, it wasn't long before we . . . Well, yes." (A lifetime habit of reticence is hard to break.) As she remembers it, she and Luddy were "separated" at the time, though she can't recall any actual discussion of the matter. Perhaps she was the only one who considered them separated. Back in New York, he still ate his dinner alone and tinkered with his model trains and waited.

The Hepburn-Harding-Hayward menage was an odd arrangement. Kate and Laura Harding had rented a rather dismal ranch house in Coldwater Canyon and moved in together, triggering a persistent rumor that Kate was a lesbian. In December, she began work on *Christopher Strong*, a film about an Amelia Earhart–ish pioneer woman aviator; it was directed by one of the few women directors in town,

Leland Hayward, Hepburn's agent and lover.

Dorothy Arzner, with whom Kate had a bit of a power struggle. Kate worked hard, and on weekends she and Laura embarked on rather childish escapades, like breaking into empty houses for the fun of it. And whenever he was in town, Leland Hayward slept over.

He was a dedicated party-goer, feeding on gossip and society.

Kate, who despised dining out and always went to bed early, made her dinner at home, read over her lines for the next day, and retired. In the small hours Leland came to wake her and share the gossip he'd harvested. If Kate seemed always isolated from the theater and film worlds around her, it may be because she met few people if she was always asleep before the party started. She made five movies in just over a year, and she was usually on the set at 6 A.M.

In February, with *Christopher Strong* finished, Kate went east to face Luddy, but somehow nothing was said, nothing was settled. Her family still thought her career foolish and boring; they still found Luddy sweet. When she went back to start work on *Morning Glory*, Luddy saw her off, promising to wait for her forever.

In later life she told an interviewer, "I disobey rules that I happen to think are silly, but I obey rules that are absolutely necessary to maintain a civilized standard of behavior." Fidelity to a husband so far away, so uncomplaining, so all-forgiving must have been one of the silly rules.

Hayward had advised her not to take the part of the conceited young actress in *Morning Glory*, but Kate was not to be pushed around just because he was her agent, and in her bed. She was right; this film was to win her her first Academy Award.

In the years before she knew Spencer Tracy, Kate was always more professional than romantic, and the Hayward romance didn't slow down her career. George Cukor directed her next film, *Little Women*, in which she played Jo as an independent modern spirit like her aunt Edith. She and Cukor became great friends over a series of projects that also included *A Bill of Divorcement*, *Sylvia Scarlett*, *Holiday*, *The Philadelphia Story*, *Keeper of the Flame*, *Adam's Rib*, *Pat and Mike*, and, in her triumphant later years, *The Corn Is Green* and *Love Among the*

Ruins. During the filming of *Little Women*, she went often to his house to swim naked in his pool, and he introduced her there to the stars of the day.

The irrepressible Tallulah Bankhead sneered at her scruples and called her a New England spinster; Kate was shocked by Bankhead's foul language. However, the tale is told that when Tallulah saw a rough cut of *Little Women*, she burst into tears and went down on her knees in homage to Kate. (This is hard to imagine; perhaps she'd been drinking.) Cukor, too, was delighted with Kate in the picture and said she cast over the whole film a "kind of power that dominated even those scenes she's not in."

Little Women was a solid box-office hit that went on to break records. After that came Kate's last commitment to RKO, *Spitfire*, an odd choice in which she played a passionately religious Ozark hillbilly. By this time she wanted more Broadway and signed on to do *The Lake* for producer Jed Harris. Back in New York, she rented a brownstone on East 49th Street, in Turtle Bay Gardens. Luddy, of course, moved in, too.

Nicknamed "The Vampire," Jed Harris was a Broadway producer whose string of smash hits had landed him on the cover of *Time* and whose personal appeal left much to be desired. Noel Coward called him a praying mantis. Ben Hecht called him Dracula. Laurence Olivier modeled his sinister Richard III on him. Harris decided to direct *The Lake* himself, and in rehearsals he shattered Kate, abusing and scolding and mocking her. For all her cocky back talk, her confidence in her own performances was fragile, and she was at the same time demoralized with indecision over a personal crisis: Leland Hayward now wanted to marry her.

Perhaps it was true love; perhaps a secret affair simply didn't feed his vanity as a public marriage would. Shuttling back and forth between Hollywood and the East, in Kate's New York

◆ MORNING GLORY ◆

HEPBURN WON AN ACADEMY
AWARD FOR HER PERFORMANCE
AS EVA LOVELACE.

Though Hollywood kept calling her gangling and horse-faced, *Morning Glory* offers us a curiously demure Hepburn, with overtones of Judy Garland. Her character, starry-eyed and stagestruck Eva Lovelace, comes to New York from a tiny town in Vermont determined to play Shakespeare and George Bernard Shaw. The role is sometimes described as that of a conceited "society girl" who needs to learn humility, but on the contrary, Eva arrives penniless, friendless, and apparently family-less. Her coat isn't warm enough, and she seems to be living under a bridge.

Talkative and self-confident, Eva barges into the waiting room of a producer named Easton (played by Adolphe Menjou, looking like a penguin), who's casting a new play, *Blue Skies*, by Joseph Sheridan. Eva gets herself introduced to Sheridan (Douglas Fairbanks Jr., who looks like a small-town Greek god and makes a most implausible playwright), and it turns out he's a fellow fan of Mr. Shaw.

Easton has nothing for her, and

she can't leave him her address and phone number because apparently she has neither. After the opening of *Blue Skies*, she crashes the party at Easton's fancy apartment, where she pretends not to be hungry though it seems she hasn't eaten in days. Downing too much champagne on an empty stomach, she waxes dramatic and plunges into Hamlet's soliloquy. This doesn't sit well with the party-goers, so she drapes herself in a tablecloth and does Juliet's balcony scene, with a fascinated Sheridan chiming in as Romeo. Then she falls asleep on Easton's lap and has to be carried upstairs to bed. There's a coy suggestion that Easton visits her there later.

Whatever happened, Eva waltzes down in the morning glowing and none the worse for wear; she and Easton are in love, she thinks, and are going to do beautiful things together—never mind that he seems to have left town and won't see her. Waiting undismayed, she takes jobs in stock, vaudeville, and nightclubs until Sheridan picks her to understudy prima donna Rita Vernon in his classy new production, *The Golden Bough.*

Just before the curtain on opening night, Rita suddenly turns vicious and holds Easton up for half the profits, a run-of-play contract, and anything else that isn't nailed down. Easton and Sheridan call her bluff, and she stalks out. Sheridan drags Eva out of the bowels of understudydom, she goes on in Rita's place, and is, unsurprisingly, a howling hit, though the movie never actually shows her on stage or shows anything of the play.

After her great moment, she tells Easton she's in love with him, but he thrusts her aside and says that to him she's nothing but "a valuable piece of theater property." Suddenly mere success seems but an empty shell as she faces a lonely life without the penguin-shaped producer. She cries hysterically, "I'm not afraid! I'm not afraid!" Nor is the audience, since obviously the handsome playwright is waiting in the wings.

Katharine Hepburn's performance in this witless confection beat May Robson in *Lady for a Day* and Diana Wynyard in *Cavalcade* for the Academy Award. It wasn't Hollywood's finest year. *The New York Herald Tribune* called her "cinema's wonder girl," but Frank S. Nugent in *The New York Times* said she gave him the jitters, with the scurrying way she walked and her breathless soulful voice.

house he kept stumbling over Luddy. Hayward nagged her to divorce him. Kate's serious-minded parents, unimpressed by the glib and indolent Hollywood boyfriend and his diamond cuff links, stuck by Luddy. Starting with her earliest teenage callers, he was the only man of Kate's they would ever like. This goes far to explain her forbearance with the husband who wouldn't leave her, for he must have been irritating to have around at times.

By the time the play opened, she was in nervous tatters.

The Lake, which had been a hit in London, concerned a young woman whose husband drowns almost immediately after the wedding ceremony, leaving her smitten with guilt. The part called for a passively tragic heroine drenched in pathos— hardly anyone's description of Kate. The play opened first in the National Theater in Washington. The Hepburns made the journey to see it, even though it meant Dr. Tom would have to spend the night in Edith's house; the two had not made peace.

The theater was standing room only, with a glittering crowd of celebrities in evening dress. Kate trudged gamely through her part, and the reviews weren't as bad as might have been expected. Her only pleasant memory of the time, however, was having tea alone with Franklin D. Roosevelt in the White House. He told her he'd seen some of her movies but couldn't make it to the play, and would she please make a movie of a favorite story of his by Kipling? She forgot the name of the story, but remembered the president as relaxed, charming, and fun. It was the last bright spot for quite a while.

The Lake opened in New York on December 26, 1933. Kate sleepwalked through it like a robot, her voice getting steadily higher and shriller as it always did under pressure. The reviews were blistering. One called her hysterical. Brooks Atkinson of *The New York Times*, lofty monarch of the theater critics,

With Douglas Fairbanks Jr. in 1933.

sneered that movie successes were all very well but stage work required talents of a higher order. Dorothy Parker fired off her famous zinger, "She ran the gamut of emotion from A to B," and all the newspapers in the land quoted it gleefully.

At the same time the situation with Luddy had come, if not to a boil, at least to a head. He moved out of her house and into the house right behind it, where he could see into her windows. When Kate needed him to repair the plumbing, he popped right over. Simultaneously Mrs. Hepburn, always referred to in headlines as Kate's mother, was appalling the world by speaking before Congress in favor of legalized birth control. This posed the very real threat of a public boycott of Kate's pictures.

On the upside, however, *Little Women* was still raking it in at the box office and, finally, after fifty-five performances, *The Lake* was put out of its misery on February 10. During its run, Kate had been taking voice lessons and studying hard. She felt that, though the play was perishing, her own performance had improved.

Then Harris dropped his bombshell: Short of money, he was taking the poor lame production on the road. They were off to Chicago, hoping to cash in on *Little Women*'s popularity in the hinterlands. Kate was frantic. She offered him all the money

As Jo (second from right) in Little Women.

she had—$13,675.75—to buy out her contract. He accepted. She was free of Harris, though not of Luddy.

She decided to spend a month or two in France to think things over. When reporters and photographers found her with the news that she'd won an Academy Award for *Morning Glory* the night before, she was already onboard the *Paris*. She fled to her stateroom and locked herself in.

Four days after she landed in France, she sailed for home again. She'd decided on divorce.

Again, her memory later played tricks on her. In *Me*, she remembers the divorce as happening earlier, much earlier, before *The Lake*, perhaps at the start of her affair with Hayward. And she remembers getting it, not to marry Hayward, but to relieve Luddy of cuckoldry. Clearly her conscience slept uneasily, so she edited the past; if she hadn't been still married to Luddy when she slept with Hayward, then she couldn't have been unfaithful.

In April of 1934 Kate went to Merida, Mexico, with Laura Harding for company, and filed for divorce. Luddy had generously given her a petition asking the court to forgo the waiting period afterward, so that she could marry Leland at once. Leland and Lola were divorced in Juarez, Mexico. Everyone waited for the wedding, but Kate stalled. When she took Leland to visit her family at Fenwick, there was Luddy as always, waiting with his camera.

Marriage to Luddy had certainly not been marriage in any usual sense, but Kate knew quite well from watching her parents what a proper marriage involved. There was no way to know in advance what Hayward would expect from a wife, but it would surely be more than bed privileges.When she went back west with a new six-picture contract with RKO, she still hadn't committed herself to a wedding date.

circa 1938

CHAPTER FIVE

INTO THE PITS AND OUT AGAIN

———◆———

In Hollywood in the mid-1930s, two female stars, poles apart, blazed at the peak of their careers. On the one hand was Mae West, lecherous and curvaceous, pushing the censorship envelope with innuendos in *She Done Him Wrong*, *I'm No Angel*, *Belle of the Nineties*, *Goin' to Town*, and *Klondike Annie*. Long before she became a joke, West was hailed as the first authentic American folk heroine since Betsy ("and all she ever made was a flag") Ross. Half the country adored her; the other half thought she was a menace to American family values and instead adored wee Shirley Temple, the dimpled darling. In 1934 alone, Temple charmed the country with *Stand Up and Cheer*, *Now and Forever*, *Little Miss Marker*, *Baby Take a Bow*, and *Bright Eyes*, winning a special Academy Award for outstanding contribution—not to mention stamina.

Between takes on the poorly received The Little Minister.

Was there a space somewhere in the gulf between West's smoldering curves and *Curly Top*'s innocent dimples for the coolly aristocratic bones of Katharine Hepburn? The prospects looked dim, and they were.

Thanks to Hayward's negotiations, Kate was making more

money than President Roosevelt, and the studio was most anxious for a return on its investment. *The Little Minister*, with Kate absurdly cast as the gypsy Lady Babbie, was a dismal flop. Early in 1935 she made *Break of Hearts* with Charles Boyer, at the time Mr. Sex himself, and rumors promptly put them in bed together, though she herself says that her efforts in that direction were unsuccessful. *Hearts* did almost as badly as *Minister*. *Alice Adams*, in spite of Kate's running battle with director George Stevens, fared better, winning her an Academy Award nomination for its small-town, social-climbing heroine, but it was followed by the disastrous *Sylvia Scarlett*. Possibly Kate took this role because it gave her a chance to wear trousers; Sylvia dresses as a boy to help her con-man father. It was supposed to be hilarious, but at the preview nobody laughed, and when the lights went up whole rows of seats had emptied. *Time* declared that "Katharine Hepburn is better looking as a boy than a woman," but that didn't help at the box office; in fact, the public held it against her, along with her mother's unladylike causes. Katharine Hepburn's star was slipping, and her next three films, *Mary of Scotland*, *A Woman Rebels*, and *Quality Street*, all costume dramas, nearly finished her off.

And to complicate the Hayward situation, John Ford came onto the scene to direct her as Mary, Queen of Scots.

The Maxwell Anderson play, *Mary of Scotland*, had been critically hailed on Broadway, and Kate was eager to play the part Helen Hayes had originated onstage. Ford was perhaps not the best choice to direct. Forthrightly macho, he used women in his films, as Kate later complained, purely for decoration. In his hands the strong role of the queen dwindled into helpless femininity— "she was a bit of an ass," Kate said. Kate might have fought Ford over the characterization, but

JOHN FORD, MELANCHOLY GENIUS

The man who was to become one of the all-time greatest movie directors was born Sean Aloysius O'Fearna—anglicized to Feeney—youngest of thirteen children (which made Mrs. Hepburn raise her eyebrows) of an Irish Catholic family. He directed his first film, *Straight Shooting*, in 1917, and by the time he tackled *Mary of Scotland* he was forty and his career was considered at its pinnacle. Nobody knew that the future would bring such classics as *Stagecoach*, *The Grapes of Wrath*, *How Green Was My Valley*, *She Wore a Yellow Ribbon*, and *The Searchers*, for a grand total of six Academy Awards.

Ford had what people who worked with him described as an almost mystical affinity for actors. He seemed to tell them wordlessly how to play a scene, and they understood. People obeyed Ford instinctively. He was an arresting presence on the set, tall and red-haired, in filthy tennis shoes, a crumpled felt hat, and a tweed jacket covered with ashes from the pipe that rarely left his mouth. He often forgot to wear socks and sometimes held his flannel trousers up with a necktie instead of a belt. When the shooting was going badly he gnawed through his pipe stem, bit holes in his handkerchief, and reduced such stalwarts as John Wayne to tears.

Ford had a sharp eye for talent. Spotting a young man named Duke Morrison, former football player for the University of Southern California, carrying props around on the Fox lot, Ford decided he'd make a good cowboy actor. He did, and as John Wayne, he went on to become an American folk hero and lifelong friend of Ford's.

In 1930, when he was casting a jailhouse drama, *Up the River*, John Ford went to Broadway in search of a star. When he saw *The Last Mile*, with Spencer Tracy giving his trademark controlled, understated performance, Ford looked no further. Tracy, another red-headed Irishman, was only thirty, but already his face was the web of anxious lines that would endear him to millions. He was married and had a six-year-old son (who was, to Tracy's great grief, deaf), but he was rarely home at night. All his life Tracy suffered from insomnia, and he prowled the city in the small hours, drinking and stopping in at brothels, where he was known as a mean and sometimes violent drunk. Deeply insecure, he accepted Ford's offer gloomily, expecting, as he always did, to fail.

In Hollywood, Ford took good care of his protégé and welcomed him into the close-knit group of actor friends with whom Ford drank and made his movies. His gang was Ford's emotional sustenance. Like Tracy, Ford was not happily married. His wife, Mary, was a tough-minded, hard-drinking former Army psychiatric nurse before whom even his manliest friends trembled with apprehension. She was determined not to let him go. Not to Katharine Hepburn, whom she despised; not to anyone.

There seems no doubt that Ford and Kate were deeply in love, even though he never could make the conscience-rending break with his wife. Probably, being a darkly complicated man himself, he responded to Kate's clarity, her quick honest temper, her optimism, and her open love for her roots and her family. And he seems to have brought out

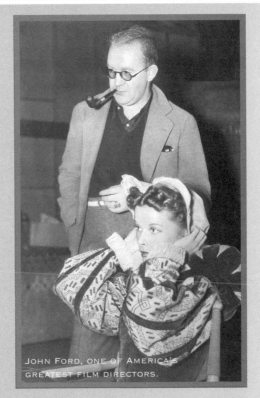

JOHN FORD, ONE OF AMERICA'S GREATEST FILM DIRECTORS.

in her a poetic, dreamy side nobody else had explored.

Over the years they were never quite free of each other. They wrote and phoned each other until he died. *Mary of Scotland* was the only film they made together, but for the rest of his long life Ford never gave up trying to work with her again, spend time with her again, even if it meant —as it would—conceding the lion's share of her attention to Spencer Tracy, the man he himself had brought to town.

unfortunately for the film she fell in love with him instead. He didn't like people to talk back to him, so she let him have his directorial way—in all but one small matter.

To the despair of directors, Kate always resisted letting anyone more dispensable take the dangerous risks in her movies. When the script called for Mary to run down a flight of stairs, wearing high heels and an enormous heavy gown, then leap onto the back of a horse and gallop away at breakneck speed, she insisted on doing it herself, over Ford's furious protests. Finally he gave in, but he paid her back by reshooting the scene eleven times. When he relented and dismissed her, the entire crew applauded wildly.

On the set they teased each other constantly. Ford told her, "You're a fine girl. If you'd just learn to shut up and knuckle under, you'd probably make somebody a nice wife." Off the set, they played golf together for a hundred dollars a hole. They sailed together on Ford's yacht, the *Araner*, his transportation to his famous drinking bouts in Mexico. He was originally from Maine, and the two shared a Yankee work ethic and affinity for boats and open water. Kate deferred to him as she later would to Tracy and massaged his feet. Playing tomboy, she fit in easily with his manly cronies.

It was Ford's custom to take time out between pictures to get long and seriously drunk, but after *Mary of Scotland* he went to Fenwick with Kate instead. A surprisingly learned and thoughtful man with an interest in politics, he and Mrs. Hepburn found common ground at once, though Dr. Tom disapproved of him as a married man up to no good.

Ford was a Catholic, but he and his wife, Mary, hadn't been married in the church because she was divorced. Now he was hoping his unhappy marriage could be escaped. He didn't want a mere affair with Kate; he wanted to marry her.

Hepburn's Academy Award did not guarantee box-office success for her follow-ing films. The dismal reception for Mary of Scotland *was more typical.*

In private she called him by his Irish name, Sean. They talked wistfully of going to Ireland together, sailing around the remote Aran Islands. In later life she said he understood her better than anyone ever did, but admitted that she never understood him. An earthy, uncomplicated person and, at least on the surface, disinclined to brood, she was as fascinated by Ford's interior darkness as she would be by Tracy's. Her own problems could usually be treated with chocolates and maple-walnut ice cream, a freezing-cold shower, and eighteen holes of golf. Ford, like Tracy, used rivers of whiskey. It didn't work.

Mary Ford intended to be Mrs. John Ford forever, and she dug in her toes and stood firm. Ford adored his fourteen-year-old daughter, Barbara, and his wife held her as her trump card: Divorce me and Barbara's mine. A niece of Ford's has said that

Kate offered Mary $150,000 in return for the divorce and the daughter, too, but Mary was adamant.

The flagrantly expensive *Mary of Scotland* was a dud at the box office. So was Kate's next picture, *A Woman Rebels*. Its successor, *Quality Street*, lost $248,000.

Halfway through making that film, Kate heard on the radio that Hayward, at last tired of waiting, had married Margaret Sullavan. She was furious, though their relationship had been essentially dead for a long time. According to popular legend, Leland Hayward was famously endowed physically, but good sex and easy conversation apparently hadn't been enough to sustain her interest. Perhaps she needed the continuing challenge that Tracy would offer her, the daily struggle with a dangerously difficult mate, to hold her attention for long.

So with Hayward gone, nothing settled between her and Ford, and a growing Hollywood reputation as box-office poison, Kate went back east to star in the Theater Guild production of *Jane Eyre*, Ford's photograph propped on her dressing-room table.

Jane Eyre is everyone's classic example of a mousy frump, but Kate had other ideas about her. With her relationship with Ford uppermost in her mind, she played Jane as spunky, fearless, and independent. In the beginning, Theater Guild producers Lawrence Langner and Teresa Helburn worried about Hepburn's ability to develop a character through three acts, a task quite different from bits-and-pieces movie work, but she enjoyed the challenge and worked hard on her performance.

With no close ties to anyone in the cast, Kate was lonely. She wrote long letters to Ford, addressing them to the studio to avoid Mary's well-known wrath. During the Boston tryout she accepted dinner invitations from millionaire producer and aviator Howard Hughes. Of all the men who passed through Kate's early life, Hughes is perhaps the oddest choice of all.

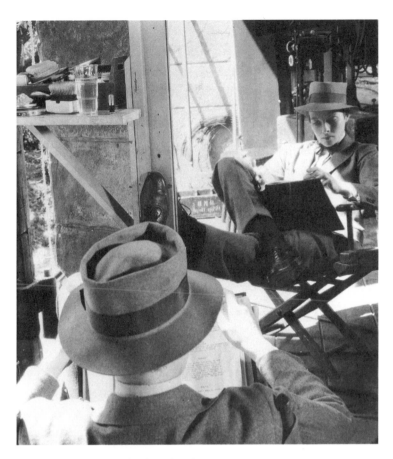

Studying the script of Sylvia Scarlett.

She was an odd choice for him, too, as he was known for his fondness for a generous bosom, never Kate's strong point.

The man who would become an eccentric billionaire recluse, self-isolated by his morbid horror of germs, first landed in her life when his plane dropped in on the *Sylvia Scarlett* location; he and her costar Cary Grant were friends, and Grant introduced them. Since then Hughes had been, literally, hovering around. Tall and stooped, with paper-white skin, he was quite deaf, which led him to avoid conversation and drop into long silences, except when the subject was airplanes. At the time he held the world record for a transcontinental flight, nine hours and twenty-seven minutes in his *Winged Bullet*. A few weeks after the Boston dinners, in January, he broke his own record, flying from Burbank to Newark in seven hours and twenty-eight minutes. He carried his triumph straight to Kate, who was in Chicago with *Jane Eyre*, the guild having decided against New York just yet. Hughes joined her at her hotel.

The famous are rarely allowed much privacy. Two days later the Los Angeles papers were splashing headlines of their impending marriage. Stung but trying to laugh it off, Ford wrote Kate a long comic letter pretending to be a sailor whose fiancée has betrayed him. *Jane Eyre* moved on to St. Louis and he called her there, but she had no way to return his calls while he was home with his wife. A series of attempts to get in touch resulted in disastrous confusion. Finally, Ford wrote her, for the first time, a genuine and moving letter of love. Kate was ecstatic. All would be well, he would leave Mary, and they would be together.

Then he wrote again, and again he was unsure of his plans.

When the play closed in Baltimore, Kate, who always despised ostentation and opulence, sailed to Nassau with Hughes on his ostentatiously opulent yacht. When she got back to Los Angeles, she told Ford she had to have a definite yes or no. He still couldn't answer. She moved into Hughes's vast and dismal house.

It seems a peculiar gesture for a woman presumably in love. Was she trying to push Ford into a decision? Was she at all attached to Hughes? Coyly, in *Me*, she says, "We had a very pleasant life. . . . It certainly was always exciting." Sometimes they flew a seaplane and landed in Long Island Sound, to dive off the wing and swim naked. He taught her to fly, and once she took off under the 59th Street Bridge. She took him to Fenwick for the usual inspection by her family, and by her ex-husband, who followed them around the golf course with his movie camera. "He is part of the family," Dr. Tom told Hughes sternly.

➤ ➤ ➤

". . . he'll cut you down to size."

This odd couple, with little in common but a taste for golf and adventures and their lofty positions on the celebrity food chain, stayed more or less together for several years. And Kate kept working, trying to haul her career back on track again. When she started *Stage Door*, she was in seventieth place in a box-office popularity poll.

In *Stage Door*, she plays yet another aspiring actress, this time rich and snooty. In America during the Depression, anyone who looked rich and snooty needed to get humbled, and Kate's character did, realizing at the end that she was no better than anyone else. It seemed that the worst might be over; *Life* magazine wrote, "Miss Hepburn really is, as her early pictures indicated, potentially the screen's finest actress." She let herself look forward to playing the most hotly contested role being cast that year, Scarlett in *Gone With the Wind*.

With Cary Grant, she launched into *Bringing Up Baby*, a farce about an heiress with a pet leopard and the zoologist she has her eye on. The movie is now a comedy classic, but at the time such romps were out of favor with the public, and so were Katharine Hepburn and any other woman who looked inde-

Though she had understudied the lead on Broadway, Hepburn starred in the movie version of Holiday.

pendent and strong. The Independent Theatre Owners Association published a list of the loved and the hated: The loved ones were adorable Shirley Temple, perky Deanna Durbin, and Fred Astaire's dancing partner Ginger Rogers; of the hated, Hepburn's name led all the rest.

Bringing Up Baby lost $365,000.

The studio was in despair. Quite possibly to get rid of her, they offered her a third-rate vehicle called *Mother Carey's Chickens.* Kate refused it and was forced to buy out her contract for $220,000, to the delight of the studio executives.

With help from her admirer, George Cukor, who had made her a star in *Little Women*, Kate landed the lead in Columbia's remake of *Holiday*, the role she had understudied so long and fruitlessly for Hope Williams in New York. Again, her reviews were good. Again, her box office was bad. The timing was off.

It had been a smash on Broadway in madcap 1928, but ten years later who would give up a good job, as Cary Grant's character in the film does, to wander around seeing the world? Who, as Hepburn's character, Linda Seton, does, would give up a gilded life to join him?

Columbia didn't suggest doing another Hepburn picture. She still hoped for Scarlett O'Hara, in spite of Selznick's low opinion of her appeal. She went, as she always did in times of stress, back to Fenwick to lick her wounds and wait for Selznick's final decision.

Just as she was leaving for the East, the Academy Awards were announced. Kate hadn't been nominated, but the Best Actor award went to Spencer Tracy as the fisherman in *Captains Courageous*. He wasn't at the banquet to receive the award; he was in the hospital for hernia surgery. Convinced that Fredric March would win it for *A Star Is Born*, he worried about how his face would look when he heard he'd lost, so he persuaded his doctor to schedule the vaguely planned elective surgery for the night of the awards. His wife graciously received it for him.

Kate must have been pleased. She had never met Tracy, but she said she had seen the movie fifty-two times and cried every time he went down with his ship.

She spent the whole summer at Fenwick. Hughes came to visit and was not a success, tying up the bathroom and complaining about the food and the shortage of hot water. Elsewhere, the playwright Philip Barry was writing a new play.

Kate swam and played golf, sometimes thirty-six holes a day. She wrote long letters to Ford. She waited to hear from Selznick, her heart so strongly set on Scarlett that she could imagine no other next move for her career.

Hughes still claimed he wanted to marry her, but he was

unfaithful whenever he got a chance and had once sailed off for two weeks with Luise Rainer, leaving Kate alone in his house. Now he was setting out on a round-the-world flight that he said was inspired by and dedicated to Kate; he promised to dip his wings when he passed over Fenwick. She packed him a bag of sandwiches for the trip and he took off, dipping as promised; the romantic gesture made all the evening news broadcasts. He set a new globe-circling record of three days, nineteen hours, and seventeen minutes, and when he came back to New York, millions cheered him at a ticker-tape parade. He was for the moment the most famous man in the country.

Philip Barry finished his new play. It was called *The Philadelphia Story*. He had written it for the very woman he'd told was too vicious to play comedy—for now he had found the key to using her.

Kate loved the play and hesitated only in hopes of hearing from Selznick. She continued to believe until December that she was perfect for Scarlett. Finally the word came. Selznick wrote, rather pompously, "Hepburn has two strikes against her—first, the unquestionable and very widespread intense public dislike of her at this moment, and second, the fact that she has yet to demonstrate the sex qualities that are probably the most important of all the many requisites of Scarlett." With the success of *The Philadelphia Story* following so promptly, Kate never bore a grudge about *Gone With the Wind*. Much later, in fact, when Selznick's eventual choice, Vivien Leigh, was trembling on the edge of a nervous breakdown, it was Kate who rushed to her support and supervised her care.

For many of Kate's older admirers, *The Philadelphia Story* was and still is the play and movie that defined and crystallized her. Katharine Hepburn, in the public mind, was Tracy

Lord. It was her sixteenth play and her sixteenth movie, but the world behaved as if she had sprung newborn from Barry's pen. The problem with her aristocratic air was resolved by making her a ditzy aristocrat, a bossy Bryn Mawr graduate who nevertheless likes to take her clothes off when she's had too much champagne. The story, as almost everyone knows by now, concerns a wealthy suburban Philadelphia family whose well-guarded privacy is invaded by a snoopy magazine reporter. There are strong overtones here of the Hepburns themselves, including even an ex-husband who keeps hanging around à la Luddy.

The Theater Guild agreed to produce the play, and Howard Hughes gave Kate $30,000 to nail down the movie rights at once. After considerable trouble with script revisions, *The Philadelphia Story*, with Van Heflin and Joseph Cotton as the

As Main Line heiress Tracy Lord in The Philadelphia Story.

THE DICK HEPBURN PROBLEM

After Kate's younger brother Dick graduated from Harvard in 1933, he announced that he wanted to write plays. Dr. Tom, perhaps by now weary of battling his children, agreed to subsidize him while he tried. Dick managed to get one play, *Behold Your God*, produced at Jasper Deeter's prestigious little Hedgerow Theater in Pennsylvania. He tried hard to use his sister's fame to promote it, but the reviews were terrible and there were no offers to take it to New York.

KATE'S YOUNGER BROTHER, DICK.

By the summer of 1938, the summer Howard Hughes visited Fenwick, Dick was twenty-six and hadn't had anything else produced, though he seemed to keep writing and pestering producers, and Kate gave him $125 a month for an apartment in New York. Jasper Deeter, who thought history was poison, turned down Dick's drama *Cortez, Conqueror of Mexico*, but encouraged his plans to write

about something he knew firsthand: Fenwick and his family.

Dick began work. Even after the hurricane of 1938 destroyed the house, his room with the notes for his play floated safely half a mile away and the notes survived. When *The Philadelphia Story* was seven months old and still going strong, in October of 1939, Dick dropped his bombshell and showed his sister his new play, *Sea-Air*.

Set during the previous summer's visit from Howard Hughes, *Sea-Air* was Fenwick and the Hepburn family to the life. The whole clan was there, artfully re-created, but especially Hughes. Hughes, who after all had bought Kate the rights to *The Philadelphia Story*, was portrayed as a loathsome character, rude and dirty. There were insulting reflections of Philip Barry, author of her current success, and Leland Hayward as well. Dick had been taking copious notes.

Kate was hysterical with rage. She had been spied on by the brother whose allowance she paid, and he was going to ruin her career. The rest of the family took her side. Dick was astonished. It was, he insisted, a comedy, not a tabloid exposé, and his portrait of Kate as the actress heroine would actually burnish her reputation. Besides, why shouldn't an artist like himself write about his surroundings; whose material was it, anyway?

Dick appealed to Jasper Deeter, going down to visit the Hedgerow Theater himself. And Deeter loved *Sea-Air*. He wanted to stage it.

Kate protested with wild tears; she was so upset she threw up. She raged that Dick and Deeter between them were out to ruin her. Hughes and Barry would desert her. Dr. Tom roared at Dick; Mrs. Hepburn implored and reasoned. There were threats to expel him from the family home without a penny.

Outgunned, Dick wrote to Deeter withdrawing the play. But he brooded. Months went by, and then suddenly, secretly, he sent the manuscript to fifteen Broadway producers. All of them turned it down. The Theater Guild's Lawrence Langner wrote Dick quite sharply, saying they would never do anything to hurt a good person like Kate.

But Deeter still believed in the play, and in Dick, which cheered him up. He went on writing and privately believing that Kate and the rest of the family had torpedoed his one big chance at fame and fortune.

The family boat had been strenuously rocked, but it didn't capsize. Decades later, Dick and Kate would share the house at Fenwick. While she still lived in the Turtle Bay house in Manhattan, she and her secretary, Phyllis Wilbourn, drove up to Fenwick almost every weekend. Dick, the might-have-been-famous playwright, entertained his friends around a table at one end of the big kitchen while Kate, the very famous actress, chatted with Phyllis as they cooked their dinner at the other end.

reporter and the ex-husband, went into tryouts in New Haven, Philadelphia, Baltimore, Washington, and Boston, and then opened in New York, at the Shubert Theater on West 44th Street. There was general apprehension among the cast, but they needn't have worried. The material was fresh, witty, and sophisticated, and Kate was superb. Even her old nemesis, the *Times*'s Brooks Atkinson, was charmed. Kate, he said, had overcome her previous stage problems and now acts "like a woman who has at last found the joy she has always been seeking in the theater."

Kate played Tracy Lord on Broadway for a year, then broke off the national tour to make the movie, at MGM. Though her original choices for costars were Clark Gable and Spencer Tracy, she ended up with Cary Grant and James Stewart instead. It's impossible to imagine the movie that might have been made with her first picks. Perhaps it would have been less lighthearted; perhaps the sheer weight of Gable and Tracy would have diminished Hepburn. At any rate, she and Tracy would have met a year earlier.

The opening scene sets the tone for many a Hepburn movie to come. Throwing her first husband out of the house, she pitches his possessions after him, first extracting a golf club from his bag of clubs, breaking it over her knee, and throwing the pieces at him. Quick as a wink, he puts his hand in her face and pushes her over backward through the door. She's a spitfire, this woman, but not to worry: A man will always have the last word. With help from rivers of champagne and a skinnydip with James Stewart, she realizes her flaws, her lack of womanly understanding and forgiveness, the fool she's been. (Her flinch when the sunshine on her wedding day strikes her smack in the hangover, though perhaps meant as a metaphor for seeing the light, is a lovely piece of business.)

Here was a Hepburn the world could love, all blue-blooded arrogance humbled and a promise of a meeker future. For whatever reasons, the Grant-Stewart-Hepburn chemistry worked, and worked triumphantly. The movie broke box-office records, earning $1.3 million.

Kate's return to Hollywood was a triumph. Now she could write her own ticket. She found a script she liked, *Woman of the Year*, about a romance between a classy lady foreign correspondent and an uncouth sportswriter, and held the studio up for a tidy fortune for it. She got George Stevens to direct. And again, she wanted Spencer Tracy. Tracy, now forty-one, might not have time; he was struggling to make *The Yearling* in the stifling, mosquito-ridden swamps of Florida. However, the film ran into troubles and was canceled. Tracy was ill and covered with mosquito bites, but free.

They met for the first time by accident, outside the Thalberg Building at MGM, and the moment promptly passed into legend—with variations. Tracy and director Joe Mankiewicz were on their way to lunch when they ran into Kate. She was tall, and wearing heels; Tracy was five foot ten. As Garson Kanin tells it in *Tracy and Hepburn*, she said, "You're rather short, aren't you?" Tracy glared, and Mankiewicz said, "Don't worry, honey, he'll cut you down to size." As biographer Anne Edwards has it, Kate said, "I'm afraid I'm a little tall for you, Mr. Tracy," and Tracy himself grinned and said, "Don't worry, Miss Hepburn. I'll cut you down to my size." Kate herself, looking back at eighty, remembers she said, "I hope it doesn't bother you that I'm so tall. I'm wearing heels, but I can change them." With her usual rosy hindsight, she sees Tracy smiling and Mankiewicz getting the comeback.

Whoever said what, Tracy and Hepburn met in August of 1941.

circa 1942

CHAPTER SIX

TRACY TAKES CHARGE

In 1975, Kate played opposite John Wayne in *Rooster Cogburn*. One night, after she had gone to bed at eight as she usually did and Wayne had opened a bottle of tequila as he usually did, the Duke mused on his costar, saying, "Imagine how she must have been at age twenty-five or thirty. How lucky a man would have been to have found her."

Suppose it had been Wayne and not Tracy? She needed a man she found manly enough to respect, though certainly the union of the far-left Kate and the far-right Wayne would have struck sparks even hotter than those in her parents' household, where Mrs. Hepburn once threw a full pot of coffee at her husband during a political discussion.

In 1981, she made *On Golden Pond* with Henry Fonda. Fonda said the whole experience was "magical for both of us," and afterward coproducer Jane Fonda said, "I couldn't help fantasizing what would have happened if she and my dad had become lovers forty years ago, and Kate had been my mother. . . ."

What if it had been Fonda and not Tracy? Was he too much the gentleman for her? Manly, to Dr. Tom's daughter, may have meant bullying.

Perhaps the fates really meant her for John Ford, her dear "Sean," but what if he had given up his daughter to marry her? Could she respect a man who'd make such a sacrifice for her? And what if Howard Hughes had been more akin to the world she knew, or if she hadn't been so preoccupied with Ford in the Hughes years? Suppose Leland Hayward had managed to hold her interest? Certainly poor patient Luddy never could; it wasn't in him to be demanding in the way she thought proper for a man.

There's a mismatch in many of Hepburn's pictures between her obvious independent self and the plot that leaves her subservient to a man; it haunted her private life as well. She had inherited her father's strong will, but its expression was crippled by the little girl who had tried so hard to please that unpleasant man. Nature and nurture, both dealt her by the same hand, crossed swords.

In Spencer Tracy, Kate found a man pursued by the same horrors that had dogged Tommy; at least she could try to save Tracy. And she found a man as insatiably demanding as Dr. Tom; she could try to please him. And there was no question of her respect. Though she often said she found acting a trivial career, she put Tracy's talent in a class by itself.

And then there was sex. Kate had always enjoyed a good roll in the hay, but the chemistry between her and Tracy was of a different order, as strong as the chemistry between her mother and father had apparently been. It showed on the screen. In the twenty-six years of their liaison, they made only

The drama off-screen between Tracy and Hepburn was often more intense than their pairing on-screen.

nine movies together, compared to thirty-two they made apart, but the world always thought of them as a pair.

In these more freewheeling times, when a moviemaker wants to show physical attraction between two people he simply cuts straight to their naked bodies wrestling joyfully in bed, or on a beach, or under a bush. In the days of prudish censorship, sex had to be subtly suggested, and the exchanged look was an art form in itself. The leading man could become the idol of millions of women on the strength of a properly ardent gaze. The audience's imagination filled in the blanks, perhaps more passionately than today's realism allows room for. Tracy could never have been called handsome, but however tough and unsentimental his character, when he looks at Hepburn and she looks back, nobody can doubt what's happening.

They began work on *Woman of the Year* sparring and finished it teasing and razzing each other, but everyone noticed, as the days passed, a change in Kate. She seemed gentler, and her clothes improved. Tracy had a problem with women in pants, and though Kate didn't go so far as to wear a skirt, her outfits were suddenly tailored and flattering instead of ragged and baggy. Tracy was still addressing her as "Shorty" and referring to her as "the woman," but Kate was in love.

When Hepburn and Tracy collided, Kate had been involved with director George Stevens for six months or so. The marriage between Louise and Spencer Tracy was basically over, though Louise maintained a strong interest and influence in his career and always held her saintly martyrdom over his head. Tracy more or less lived at the Beverly Hills Hotel, though he visited Louise and the children regularly at their home on what he called the Hill, one of the Beverly Hills, a comfortable ranch he'd bought to have a place for his polo ponies. He seems to have been uncomfortable with his son John and blamed himself and the venereal infections he'd picked up in brothels for the boy's deafness, but he loved his daughter, also Louise, called Susie.

Tracy was, if possible, a sort of bachelor family man, and he led a bachelor life among the ladies. His affairs were apparently no more than the usual in that town at that time and didn't usually last much longer than the filming of a movie. They had included Loretta Young, Ingrid Bergman, Olivia de Havilland, Judy Garland, and quite a few others.

Now that the principals are dying off or retreating beyond the libel laws and their children are publishing tell-all books, it seems that in the century's middle decades, everyone in Hollywood was sleeping with everyone else in Hollywood. Apparently it was the local competitive sport of choice, and Leland Hayward was far from alone in his scalp collecting. Working movie actors led a strenuous life and needed to keep early hours, a clear complexion, and bag-free eyes, but somehow they found the time and energy for bed-hopping so brisk it sounds like a full-time job. The wonder isn't that so many filmland marriages ended in divorce, but that any lasted.

From the beginning there was no question as to who was in the driver's seat of the Tracy-Hepburn affair. In Hollywood, which costar gets top billing is a tensely emotional matter, the ultimate measure of one's value; in all their films, Tracy's name was on top, and no chivalrous or affectionate impulse ever moved it down.

Hepburn freely admitted that always, when change was necessary, it was she who changed; if compromises had to be made, she was the compromiser. She deferred in all matters to Tracy. She gentled her ways. She held her tongue, at least when Tracy was in earshot. Ford had found her perfect the way she was; for Tracy, everything needed changing—her voice, her clothes, her conversation, her acting, her politics, her opinions.

Woman of the Year, their first film together, reflects their own dynamics as well as the temper of the times. Tess Harding, the brilliant journalist, must be humiliated by the glaring, lowbrow Sam Craig and punished for being a career woman instead of a housewife. In the final sequence she struggles unsuccessfully to make his breakfast while he glowers at her, and the message is plain: She should have been studying not world affairs, but how to please a man.

Kate's militant mother and aunt Edith, in the expansive earlier years of the century, had never faced anything quite as repressive as the enforced domestic chatteldom of the '40s and '50s. Nobody in 1925 would have dared suggest that women had no higher calling, no greater spiritual, intellectual, or social potential than fixing a man his breakfast. Few people at mid-century would have dared suggest otherwise.

When Kate saw the ending she said it was the "worst bunch of shit I've ever read," but perhaps because of it, the movie was a great popular hit, even bigger than *The Philadelphia Story*. James Agee, in *Time*, said its stars "succeed in turning several batches of cinematic corn into passable moonshine." Critics praised Kate, saying she had finally shed her irritating mannerisms and was never better. Perhaps that was Tracy's doing; Clark Gable once said, "Nobody's better than when they act with him."

As soon as rumors of their affair began to buzz around the movie world, Ford, who had been enjoying a long, fruitful run of some of his best work, quietly packed a bag and left town. He joined the Naval Reserve and didn't come back to Hollywood until after the war. On the eve of Pearl Harbor, Mary Ford traveled to Washington to say good-bye to him. Her second ex-husband had recently died, leaving her no longer a divorcée but a widow in the church's eyes. Ford was going off to war, and apparently he felt the time was ripe to make his peace with Rome. He remarried Mary in a Catholic ceremony.

This marked the end, for Kate, of five years of wistful uncertainty. It meant Ford no longer believed they had a future together, however remote. She could turn her full attention to Tracy. Tracy, who needed attention desperately, responded.

Between 1942 and 1950, while Tracy and Hepburn made six movies together, he also made eight other movies, seven of which were considerable successes—major films that only burnished his reputation and bolstered his prices. Meanwhile Kate in the same years made only four pictures without Tracy, all of them negligible. Even in those six movies they made together, his role was always the larger.

Tracy's method of keeping the upper hand was peculiarly effective. He continued to go on binges, locking himself into his hotel room with a crate of whiskey. Whenever possible, Kate slept on the floor in the hall outside, keeping watch as she hadn't kept watch over Tommy. Sometimes, unable to bear the silence beyond the door, she would get the hotel staff to unlock it for her. Often he'd have piled a barricade of furniture against the door. She would force her way in to find him— maybe naked, maybe passed out in his own vomit, but alive, as Tommy hadn't been.

Once, when Kate left Spencer in New York to go film another forgettable movie in Hollywood, he retaliated with a record-breaking binge, winding up straitjacketed in a hospital, hallucinating wildly. Small wonder that she eventually chose no roles that would take her away from him, no matter what the cost to her career.

He drank and turned the full blast of his unhappiness on Kate. She always took it meekly, never answered back, and stayed out of the general conversation in his presence, leaving him the whole stage. She egged him on to tell the stories everyone had already heard.

Once *Woman of the Year* was finished, Kate went east for the new Philip Barry play, *Without Love*, a pre-Tracy commitment to Lawrence Langner of the Theater Guild. Tracy, back in Hollywood, was not pleased to be abandoned. Rather than beg Kate to break her commitment, he signaled his displeasure— not for the last time—by drinking his way through the filming of *Tortilla Flat*, mixing the booze into a chemical stew with

A TALENTED, DIFFICULT MAN

SPENCER
TRACY

He was born April 5, 1900, in Milwaukee, and named Spencer Bonaventure Tracy. His father, a big, proud Irishman in the trucking business, always regretted that his son didn't join him in that more fittingly manly occupation, especially since he thought Spencer was too homely ever to make a success of acting. John Tracy was a good sport about it, however; he paid the kid's tuition at acting school, and once when Tracy was on tour and played Milwaukee, his father came to see him and enjoyed his performance. "I could hear every word," he said. (Tracy was friends with the Kennedy clan; he said the whole family reminded him of his father.)

The young Tracy was a rebel and hell-raiser. At age seven he ran away from home for a whole day, and he somehow managed to get expelled from a total of fifteen grade schools before he reformed himself and decided, rather to his family's astonishment, to become a priest. Impulsively, he joined the navy instead, and for a while considered life as a sailor, but his father made him come back and finish high school. Spencer went on to Ripon College, where he argued so much he was put on the debating team, from which he drifted into the drama club.

While the debating team was traveling, he stopped off in New York, auditioned with the American Academy of Dramatic Arts, and was offered a scholarship. He took it. Later he credited his teachers there with teaching him all he knew: simplicity and honesty, with no faddish theories or arty intellectualizing.

Through the 1920s Spencer Tracy struggled to get work on Broadway, suffering the usual ups and downs until John Ford spotted him onstage and brought him to Hollywood.

Tracy took his Catholicism quite seriously and perhaps never shed his boyhood yearning for the priesthood. When he played priests, in *Boys Town, San Francisco*, and *The Devil at 4 O'Clock*, he felt mysteriously at home in the habit. It showed; he won an Academy Award for *Boys Town*.

How he coped with a quarter century of adultery must remain a secret of the confessional. Perhaps he felt that divorce would be an even darker sin.

Tracy was never an easy man to have around, professionally or personally. Insecurity bedeviled him, and even at the peak of his career he was always afraid the world would suddenly realize he was a fraud. He was a binge drinker who sometimes took, by his own admission, two-week lunch hours. Even in the years when he wasn't drinking, he would hole up from time to time and stop answering the telephone. He developed peculiar, reclusive routines. Even his best friends didn't know he smoked; nobody saw him smoke his pack-and-a-half per day, or rather per night. A lifelong insomniac, he went to bed after the eleven o'clock news with his cigarettes and murder mysteries. At other times he read widely on all subjects, but the night was for whodunits. He would get up from time to time to make more coffee, then go back to bed to read and smoke, until finally he fell asleep around dawn. He fell asleep at about the same time Kate would be getting up to swim or watch the sun rise. Perhaps it was all for the best that they never lived together, or even spent the night together; whose night would they spend?

Tracy was always fiercely critical of his friends and lovers, and his sharp wit was usually at someone else's expense, often Kate's, making her thin, freckled skin redden in front of friends or on the set. His mimicry and sarcasm were withering and his temper awe-inspiring. This man that generations thought of as a rock of reliability and common sense could fly into a four-year-old's fury, gray eyes turning almost white with rage. Those who worked with him were reverent, even idolatrous, about his talent, but they had to suffer much to remain his friends. In his last year, Garson Kanin, perhaps his closest friend, called him to chat some two hundred and fifty times. Tracy called Kanin once.

In The Dragon Seed.

chloral hydrate and barbiturates, though doctors had already warned him about his liver and kidneys.

Without Love went on its pre-Broadway tryout tour loaded with problems. Kate was distracted with worry about Tracy, as he'd intended she should be. She'd wanted him with her in the play; but the Theater Guild, worried about his boozy reputation, had cast Elliott Nugent instead, and Kate resented it. Also the plot was a hash. Barry, master of pre-war comedy, was trying and failing to write something serious for the serious new times.

Before the play was due to open on Broadway, Kate announced that she would leave the cast after the tour to go west and make *Keeper of the Flame* with Tracy. She would be back for the New York run in September.

Not if Tracy could help it, she wouldn't.

❧ ❧ ❧

"He means what he says when he says it . . ."

That summer, Kate rented a house in Malibu Beach, and she and Tracy retreated to it. During the days, they worked on *Keeper*, which was having script troubles, imperfectly integrating romance and wartime seriousness. On the set, Kate's behavior with Tracy was an embarrassment to watch. She hovered. She worshiped. She combed his hair and straightened his tie and hung on his every word. He reacted with indifference, sarcasm, and sometimes abuse. Colleagues squirmed, but Kate pretended not to mind. In the evening she took Tracy to her house, cooked his dinner, bolstered his ego, and then drove him back to his permanent suite at the Beverly Hills Hotel. Weekends, they walked on the beach and painted.

They both painted. Kate hung her productions on the walls; Tracy kept his a secret. Fanny Brice had gotten him into painting, during one of his periods of misery, saying it had done wonders for her; she sent him a kit of paints and brushes and canvases. Kate had started back in the '30s when she was having man trouble. Now they painted together, Tracy later told Garson Kanin, because they were both having man troubles— "with the same man."

All summer she kept changing her phone number and dodging questions from Barry and the Theater Guild. She wrote asking them to postpone the opening until October. Finally, in September, she wrote them again begging them to let her out of *Without Love*. For personal reasons, she couldn't possibly come east for the four months her contract called for.

Having no phone number for her, Terry Helburn of the Theater Guild went to Hollywood and found Kate. She bullied and pleaded. Kate screamed and threatened to quit acting altogether. Finally she realized she had no alternative, but declared she would stay with the play no longer than the sixteen weeks she had signed for.

Surprisingly, though the critics hated *Without Love*, audiences adored it, to the great relief of Barry and the guild. They had invested heavily in it, and now it began to make money. But Kate was adamant; February thirteenth was her last day. The play, however, had been written and produced for her, and she couldn't be replaced. Even Dr. Tom was persuaded to try to change her mind, but he too was helpless against the silent will of Spencer Tracy.

When Kate's minimum contracted time was up she walked out. She left Barry and the Theater Guild, to whom she owed so much for *The Philadelphia Story*, holding the bag. The play promptly closed. Tracy was victorious.

She was so deeply immersed in Tracy's feelings she barely noticed anyone else's. Hoping to distract him, to keep him busy, a couple of years later she persuaded Philip Barry, who was understandably astonished after what the pair had done to him, to let them make a film of *Without Love*. In 1945 she took Tracy to New York to meet with Lawrence Langner and Teresa Helburn of the Theater Guild, though they, too, had sustained losses from the production he'd persuaded her to leave.

On the same trip, she introduced him to Robert Sherwood and talked Sherwood into casting Tracy as the newspaper editor at war in his new play, *The Rugged Path*, to be produced in the fall by the Playwrights' Company. And she took Spencer to Fenwick to see her heart's home and meet her family. It was a mistake.

Later Tracy held forth at length to director Frank Capra on the visit. Accustomed to being the center of attention, he complained that the Hepburns talked all the time, without pausing to listen. He sneered at their liberal politics. He said, "Well, you know Madam Do-Gooder here. . . . Her family are all bigger fruitcakes than she is. You know—ultra-liberal New England aristocrats that work their ass off for the poor, poor folk but never see one." He was more angry than amused when Dr. Tom, defender of the unfortunate, chased away a fisherman who had sneaked through the barricades on the Hepburn beach.

For their part, the Hepburns were unimpressed to the point of boredom. They simply didn't find Spencer Tracy very interesting. And, of course, if moviemaking was a frivolous career for their daughter, it must have seemed even less worthy of a grown man's attention.

If Kate had hoped to integrate the two incompatible halves of her life, it was never to happen.

Soon after, Tracy launched into the Sherwood play *The Rugged Path*. It's impossible to know why he behaved so perversely on this project. The war was drawing to a close; Tracy admired Robert Sherwood deeply, and, in the beginning, he believed strongly in the play and in his part. He felt it would

THE COMFORT OF HOME

HEPBURN AT HOME IN
HER LATER YEARS.

Perhaps one reason Katharine Hepburn never married Spencer Tracy was that she could see quite well the problem of sharing living quarters with him. Tracy was indifferent to houses. He lived for years in a hotel, and then afterward in a small bungalow on George Cukor's property that Kate furnished with what comforts Tracy would allow. He liked confined dark places with shuttered windows and sometimes holed up in them for long stretches of time, letting his phone ring unanswered. Kate liked big bright spaces, with windows bared to the morning sun. Tracy was allergic to sun.

Tracy was a natural recluse, a lonely man given to long grim silences. Kate was raised in a house full of family and guests and casual drop-ins, all arguing at the tops of their lungs. Her house in New York's Turtle Bay was home base for any friend or relative or colleague who happened to be in town, and the door key was passed out freely to anyone who needed it.

Tracy hated traveling and rarely managed to board an airplane sober. Kate found flying as natural as walking and loved new places. Touring in plays and filming on location, she was to roam all over the United

States, England, France, Spain, Africa, Australia, Italy, and Wales.

Tracy complained that country life made him lethargic; Kate loved the country, fields, and woods. Tracy barely noticed the objects around him and said, "I don't own one damned thing I'd miss for more than five minutes if I lost it or if it were swiped." Kate loved her things.

In 1937 she had bought the Turtle Bay town house originally rented for herself and Luddy, and here and at Fenwick were where her heart and her souvenirs lived. She gardened intensively and decked both houses with fresh flowers. She cut her own firewood in Connecticut and built roaring fires in both houses. Over the years, she filled her homes with paintings and drawings and sculptures by herself and her friends, photographs of Tracy, stuffed birds, dried flowers, African masks and a chieftain's chair, Mexican and Eskimoan trinkets, her childhood ice skates, a rocking chair, part of a boat she'd once owned, wooden ducks and seagulls, wall hangings, a collection of souvenir hats, clocks and lamps and embroidered pillows, and an antique sled.

She had a kind of domestic genius. Loving food and hating restaurants, she threw herself into cooking and made the kitchen the heart of the house, with friends and staff crowding in, steaks grilling, dogs and cats underfoot. The spartan Kate of the ice-cold plunges didn't create spartan living space; it was her lusty enthusiasm for "the song of life" that spilled over into her homes.

At eighty, she told photographer John Bryson, "I've lived like a man. I've got my own house. Always have. So I haven't lived like a woman at all. I can mend anything, do all the tough work in the garden. . . ."

By this time, of course, the question of whether she had wanted to marry Tracy, to normalize their arrangement and secure their relationship, had long since ceased to matter. Probably in the early years, whatever she said for the record, she had thought about marrying Tracy—marriage, at the time, was generally considered the natural outcome of romantic love, and even the feminist Mrs. Hepburn believed it was a woman's highest calling. Certainly there were times, as when he was ill, when living together would have been convenient. But later she must have realized it was all for the best the way it was. Perhaps Kate meant just what she said—that she cherished what scraps of independence Tracy left her.

Katharine Hepburn, circa 1945.

somehow redeem him for the fact that he wasn't in uniform, something that had been eating at him deeply. His good friend Garson Kanin would be directing. And Kate would be in New

York with him. (The Theater Guild had offered her a choice of good parts while she was there, but it was clear that Tracy, agonized as always by fear of failure, would need her constantly at his side. She turned them down.)

Yet somehow, with rehearsals about to start in the fall, Tracy had failed to sign the contract, which provided that he could quit at any time with just two weeks' notice. Shortly before the first rehearsal, he suddenly demanded a share of the profits, an odd move for a man who didn't need the money and had felt so noble about the enterprise. Victor Samrock, business manager of Playwrights' Company, said no. Tracy didn't show up for the rehearsal. Sherwood told the assembled cast that the production would have to be postponed for a year until another actor could be found for the lead.

Hearing of it, Tracy apologized and said he would come to rehearsals. But he continued to shoot himself and the production in the foot. During tryouts he picked fights with everyone and kept threatening to quit; alternately, he threatened to go back on the bottle, from which Kate had temporarily separated him. She followed him around everywhere and plied him with chocolates, which she was convinced would cure the lust for liquor. He insulted Sherwood. He sneered at the play he had previously loved. In Boston, he did quit. Then he came back, but not before rumors had reached New York and torpedoed advance ticket sales.

In November the production limped onto Broadway. At the theater Kate scrubbed Tracy's dressing room and bathroom until they glittered spotlessly and brought in new curtains and rugs. In spite of Tracy's tantrums, the show did go on. Though critics didn't think much of the play, they approved of his low-key performance. The production's future might have been bright, but Tracy was bent on self-sabotage.

He kept changing his mind about when he was going to quit and, to aggravate matters, announcing his varying deadlines to the press. In December Sherwood pleaded with him to lighten the atmosphere, end the bad feeling, and commit himself firmly to a minimum of a hundred performances. Tracy turned him down. As a result, ticket sales crashed, and *The Rugged Path* closed in mid-January, leaving another playwright and another production company crushed under Tracy's temperamental wreckage.

During the war years, Tracy had found a new guilt to add to his treasury of guilts: He wasn't in the army. John Ford flew in bombers over Japanese military installations; he filmed enemy attacks under fire; he was wounded in the Battle of Midway. Not only were fellow actors James Stewart, Henry Fonda, Tyrone Power, Robert Montgomery, Robert Taylor, and Clark Gable all in uniform, so were directors such as William Wyler, Frank Capra, and even the distinctly unmacho George Cukor. Hecklers had jeered at Tracy the civilian, and Mary Ford, playing the war wife to the hilt, never missed a chance to slip her knife in.

So when John Ford came home to Hollywood a war hero, full of plans for new projects and eager as always to work with Kate, Kate understandably shied away. Ford offered her the lead in *The Ghost and Mrs. Muir*. She turned it down. She could have used a good part right then, but with Tracy on her hands she had little attention to spare for her slipping career.

Still, she had always longed to act in something more substantial than MGM fluff, and when Lawrence Langner came to Hollywood with a proposition, it must have been a sore temptation. Langner had learned from *Without Love* that if he wanted Kate in New York and on tour, the only safe thing was to have her bring Tracy, warts and all. He proposed an independent production company for the pair, with which they could spread their wings in full-bodied fare like Shaw's *The Devil's Disciple* and O'Neill's *Desire Under the Elms* while still making a movie a year in Hollywood. Kate must have been yearning to say yes— she had long wanted to do some O'Neill—but as usual she deferred to Tracy, saying, to Langner's horrified astonishment, that she was too stupid for such decisions.

Tracy said he'd think it over after he and Kate finished *The Sea of Grass*. Nothing came of it.

Everyone was braced for Tracy trouble on *The Sea of Grass*, a western about a nineteenth-century New Mexico cattle baron, but Kate was doing her work well. She had kept him sober, fattening him up considerably in the process with her sugar cure, and during the filming she shielded him fiercely from any criticism or stress that might set him off again.

Off the set, she continued to live the airless life of a married man's discreet mistress. She and Tracy saw only a few close friends, privately; to the world Louise was still very much Mrs. Spencer Tracy and Kate's status no higher than the prostitutes Tracy used to visit.

The press left them their privacy, and beyond the gossip centers of filmland few people noticed their affair. Tracy continued to visit his family on the Hill. Kate, with her strong sense of home and love of gardening, was still leading a gypsy life renting other people's houses. Before Tracy, she could consider Hollywood a workplace, visited strictly for career reasons, and Fenwick and the house at Turtle Bay her real homes. But now he had her nailed to the West, he who couldn't cope without her, and in the West she was homeless.

The question must come to mind, Why did people put up with Spencer Tracy? Kate, perhaps, had been programmed as a child to love and serve a demanding, ungrateful man and cosset his problems, but what about others? Why keep hiring and working with a bad-tempered, unreliable drunk who insulted the rest of the cast and often disappeared without notice?

The answer is that everyone admired him. It seems odd now, at the end of the century, when live theater has faded from most people's lives and movies have been taken over by special effects and megabuck stars, but there was a time when acting was considered an art. It was important. People quite unconnected with film or theater argued about techniques and theories, Lee Strasberg's The Actors Studio and its famous products, Marlon Brando and the Method.

The answer is straightforward: Spencer Tracy was simply very good at what he did. John Ford considered him the greatest actor of his day. George M. Cohan said he was "the best actor I've ever seen." Humphrey Bogart said he was by far the best living actor, with "no bullshit in it. . . . Spencer does it, that's all. Feels it. Says it. . . . He means what he says when he says it, and if you think that's easy, try it."

Jean Simmons called him "more than an actor. He's a sort of sorcerer." At its highest level there is something almost supernatural about great acting, a form of extrasensory perception. Tracy liked to brag that when he walked down the street, nobody recognized him unless he wanted them to, and apparently it was true. He could vacate his flesh at will, inhabit it or replace the inhabitant, and alter it in the eyes of an audience. As Ford, directing, could wordlessly let his actors know what he wanted, so Tracy could change his image without changing anything visible.

He hated all makeup, hated to act with anything on his face. When Kanin was directing him onstage in *The Rugged Path*, Tracy's character had to appear as though he had come direct from eight days adrift at sea. A face-piece was produced that looked like a heavy growth of beard, appropriate after a razorless week. Tracy rejected it. Kanin complained. He said, "You're not going to tell me you can act unshaven." "Watch me," said Tracy.

And director and audience looked at the clean-shaven Tracy onstage and saw a man with an eight-day growth of beard.

People put up with Tracy because, in a day when acting still mattered, he was the best.

circa 1948

CHAPTER SEVEN

BREAKING FREE

Kate found herself approaching forty. She had spent what might have been her most productive years trying to cheer up Spencer Tracy; but he remained entangled with his personal demons, and by now it was clear he would never divorce Louise. The first sign that Kate was chafing under the yoke came in 1947, when she put on a bold red dress and spoke at the rally for the Progressive Party candidate Henry Wallace, attacking the communist-hunting House UnAmerican Activities Committee that was poised to cleanse Hollywood's stable.

Tracy, contemptuous of left-wing politics, disapproved, but she spoke anyway, braving his scorn. The gesture backfired, however; conservative protestors damaged ticket sales for her next movie, *Song of Love*, in which she'd given an excellent performance as the composer Schumann's wife. Her name was turned in to the House committee as a communist sympathizer, and Louis B. Mayer rebuked her sharply. Still, the first breath of air had blown through the cage of her submission to Tracy.

Tracy, the anxious traveler, was with difficulty persuaded to go to England to film *Edward, My Son* for George Cukor, and Kate had to go with him to help him cope. There were plans, later aborted, for her to appear briefly on stage in Berlin with a reprise of *The Philadelphia Story*. On shipboard, as she read over the familiar lines, she saw how her life had bogged down and lost its forward momentum. She who loved risk and change and challenge and experiment would be repeating something she'd created ten years ago. She was stalled in the past.

Her aunt Edith, who never recovered from her surgery and had lain in a coma for seven years, died in 1948, and perhaps this too had its effect. Perhaps Kate saw herself as having also been in a coma, and one her independent aunt would have scorned.

Back in California, after she and Tracy had wrapped up *State of the Union*, Lawrence Langner—always Kate's provider of challenges—urged her to play Rosalind in *As You Like It*. Shakespeare, the ultimate challenge. Furthermore, Langner added winningly, it would give her a chance to appear in tights and show off the best-looking legs in the country.

She said yes. Knowing she still wasn't ready for Shakespeare, she arranged to coach with Constance Collier, a theatrical grande dame who, at seventy-one, had played all of Shakespeare's great women. The two became fast friends and had great fun working together. Life was opening up.

The stage, back then, conferred status. Movie stars commanding awesome salaries for a film still regularly journeyed east to take their chances with the blistering Broadway critics

On the set of State of the Union.

and sophisticated live audiences; they spent months on tour in off-Broadway spots like Cleveland, Buffalo, and Tulsa. The stage was art. Mrs. Hepburn wasn't the only person who felt that movies were a flimsy commercial imitation of the real thing.

Kate was going to take the plunge again. Her interior clock favored movie work, with its 6 A.M. makeup calls, and she struggled through the late nights of live theater; but theater, particularly Shakespeare, was a long step out into the world of risk. She was back in the land of the living, bright-eyed and gathering strength. Besides, her mother, for once, would take notice.

Simply making the decision to return to the stage energized Kate, and the energy showed in her next movie with Tracy, *Adam's Rib*, their best since *Woman of the Year*. Of course, it worked the same old territory: A strong-minded woman (this time a lawyer defending a woman who had shot her husband) faces up to a man (this time the lawyer's husband, the prosecuting attorney) and gets herself slapped down and ridiculed. In the process, equal rights for women also get slapped down and ridiculed, which at the time was a popular stance. Mrs. Hepburn, lifelong crusader, was understandably unhappy.

Then came New York and Rosalind. From the beginning there was tension between Langner, who wanted to control costs, and director Michael Benthall, who wanted a real eye-popping production with all the frills and furbelows. Kate sided with Benthall, and the result was so flossy and overblown that it irritated the critics. Brooks Atkinson sneered that it was "more showmanship than acting" and called it a "marshmallow contrivance." More kindly, he said that Kate had "too sharply defined a personality for such romantic make-believe." Howard Barnes, in *The New York Herald Tribune*, complained of Kate's "strident insistency," but the *New York Post* reviewer said he was a "longtime admirer of this frank and courageous woman" and he was proud of her. Kate sent his review to her mother.

Looking back in her memoir, she thought the critics felt she had her nerve to be attempting Shakespeare. However, the audiences disagreed and seemed perfectly happy with her— the show was virtually sold out for a hundred and thirty-eight performances.

In June *As You Like It* closed for the summer, with plans for a national tour in the fall, and Kate went back to Tracy. No doubt she worried about what he would do while she was away on tour and he was alone in his hotel room with nobody to deal with his moods. Perhaps she also felt the need to set up a kind of home, however makeshift, in which the two of them could feel more settled and rooted, even if she didn't share it with him.

She arranged with the long-suffering director George Cukor, always her great friend and admirer, to move Tracy into a cottage on his estate. Having Tracy as a tenant and acting as surrogate nurse and therapist was a heavy responsibility, but Cukor shouldered it; Kate moved her difficult lover into what would become his permanent home.

After fifteen years of rented California houses where she kept all her possessions in one bedroom, Kate naturally tried to make a nest of the cottage, to bring in flowers and pictures and souvenirs, but Tracy was adamant: no possessions, no encumbrances. The best she could manage were a few essential comforts, a reading light, and a chair in which to sit and brood. Tracy kept the door shut. Even Cukor—even Kate— needed an invitation to cross his threshold.

With Tracy settled in and supervised, Kate was free to go on tour as Rosalind, springing around in tights with her spirits restored. She had already agreed to another, more drastic separation, to film *The African Queen.* As if to signal her

On stage as Rosalind, in As You Like It.

approval of Kate's expanding horizons, Mrs. Hepburn traveled to Buffalo to catch one of her final performances. This

was serious theater; this was Shakespeare. Kate, at forty-three, had vindicated her decision to be an actress and her mother was pleased. In fact, she had gone so far as to save clippings of the reviews of *As You Like It*. She was finally proud of her daughter.

Then, quietly, she died.

Kate was visiting her parents in Hartford, and she and her father had been out for a brisk walk. Returning for the sacred family teatime, they found the table set and a pot of freshly brewed tea still hot, but no Mrs. Hepburn. After waiting for a few minutes, they called her. No answer. Together they went upstairs and found her on her bed, her body still warm to the touch, a bedsheet clenched in her hands, dead of a cerebral hemorrhage.

As it had been with Tommy, Kate's first thought was to protect her father. She sent him quickly away and arranged the body more peacefully; Dr. Tom should never suppose she suffered. Following the family custom, there was no discussion, no mourning. Dr. Tom must be allowed to ignore his wife's death as he had his son's.

Several days later Kate's brother Bob stopped in and found his father throwing out mountains of papers and letters, all Mrs. Hepburn's records of decades of battle for women's rights, suffrage, and birth control—a small library of modern women's history. Horrified, Bob asked what he was doing. "I'm throwing away all this socialist junk," said Dr. Tom. Perhaps four decades of battles over politics—the only area in which she'd resisted this man who so hated resistance—had eroded his affection for his wife. Or perhaps he had been jealous of her political passions.

Kate stayed on to arrange for the burial and her father's care in his newly single life. Tracy didn't bother to come east to help or comfort her. Perhaps he felt that a Kate in need of help and comfort was a reversal of their proper roles.

Then she sailed away. She said later, "What you do is to move along, get on with it and be tough." She refused herself the luxury of grief or remembering. In her memoir of the time, *The Making of The African Queen, or, How I Went to Africa With Bogart, Bacall, and Huston and Almost Lost My Mind*, she mentions her mother's death only once, in passing, and no one connected with her new project suspected she was under any unusual strain.

It must have drained her, this refusal to grieve. Kate had always considered herself a creature of her parents, a person who had never really left home, a woman warmed and fueled by family. In her forties, she still sent all the money she made to her father to invest for her and pay her bills; he sent her an allowance. But her mother's death revealed family to be a fragile shelter, temporary at best, and now it was crumbling.

Less than a month after Kit Houghton Hepburn died, Kate was in Liverpool on her way to Africa.

✹ ✹ ✹

"The African Queen"

From their earliest negotiations on *The African Queen*, Kate and director John Huston had put each other's backs up. He found her pushy and irritating; she kept after him to discuss the script, but he refused to be rushed. She found him unreliable and, worse, unpunctual, and she was a demon for promptness, often fondly recalling how, in her childhood, if you were two minutes late meeting Dr. Tom, he would simply drive off without you. In her memoir, she sneered at Huston's "studied

THE WATER CURE

Kate was particularly entranced by the presence of a shower at Biondo. Bathroom facilities were central to her life, and when traveling they were uppermost in her mind. Because she always drank floods of water, she needed a toilet frequently, and she was addicted to showering. At the camp, Huston had most considerately rigged up a contraption with an overhead barrel, a short pipe, and a showerhead that, when you pulled a chain, released a cupful or so of water. Pull again, another cupful. The floor was slippery mud that kept getting deeper and wetter in the equatorial damp, but Kate arranged some flooring boards so as not to leave dirtier than she'd arrived.

She doesn't say how many times a day she resorted to this sanctuary or how often the hired help had to refill her barrel. In civilized places she showered seven or eight times a day. Once, in Hollywood, when she was touring a house she was considering renting, she gave it the crucial test by taking a shower then and there. Her friends tend to gloss over this obsession, but those who had to share facilities with her, at Bryn Mawr or in summer stock, remembered it resentfully.

Garson Kanin tells the story of being present at the wedding of Laurence Olivier and Vivien Leigh. They had made plans, secret until the very night of the ceremony, to be married after midnight at Ronald Coleman's house. Kanin insisted they bring Kate along, as witness or maid of honor, because he was trying to interest her in a movie project dear to his heart.

When they got to her house she had already gone to bed, but Kanin woke her and explained. It would keep her up late, but she was game for anything and agreed to come along—if, she added, she could first take a shower. Kanin complained, pointing out that the enterprise was already running late and she would certainly have showered before she went to bed. "Yes," she said, "but I've been to sleep and now I'm up."

The proceedings were delayed so long that Coleman had to ply the preacher with strong drink to keep him from stalking out in a huff. By the time the bride and groom and freshly cleansed Kate arrived, he was drunk as a boiled owl and forgot the words to the ceremony. Not many people would jeopardize the plans of so famous a couple in order to take yet another shower, possibly her ninth of the day.

old-Kentucky-colonel charm" and said that when he was around, "everyone focuses attention on him as if there is a small child in the room."

From London, Huston went on ahead of the others, and when they arrived to meet him in what was then Stanleyville in the Belgian Congo, they found he had already left just an hour before by private plane for their camp at Biondo to check out the possibility of shooting elephants. Kate was furious. Later she grew very fond of costar Humphrey Bogart and his wife Betty, known to the world as Lauren Bacall, but at the airfield in Stanleyville Kate felt she'd been abandoned among strangers.

If the intrepid Kate was less excited about her adventure than she was furious about Huston, she must have been dodging a grief too grim to face. However, with her usual nose for a fairway, she found a primitive, tree-studded nine-hole golf course in Stanleyville and worked out her anger on it. And, always domestic and practical, she went shopping for what she would need, including stewing pots and, to come in handiest of all, a double boiler.

Filmmaking involves as much waiting around as does army life. One day Kate and the Bogarts rented a motorboat to visit a fishing village on the other side of the Congo River. Halfway across, the motor burst into flames. The boatman was hideously burned, and the boat wallowed out of control in the current. Bogart jumped into another boat to commandeer its fire extinguisher, but, perhaps like other fire extinguishers on the Congo, it turned out to be purely ornamental. Crouching down in the smoky flames, Bogart managed to smother them by hand with sand and a blanket. Then the trio maneuvered to get the burned boatman into the local hospital for blacks, though the Belgians seemed to think they were making rather a fuss about nothing.

From then on Kate was a Bogart fan. The incident had combined everything she admired most—fearlessness, resource-fulness, and concern for the unfortunate. She admired Betty, too: "I gazed at her and wondered if I should go mad with jealousy as I compared our ages—our skin—our hair—our natures." She might also have compared their menfolk. Bogie was not only a real man and a fine actor, he was, at least when sober, kind and gentle and considerate.

She lent him a tailored suit she'd brought along, and it fit perfectly. He wore it as they set out for the jungle.

The last train stop was Ponthierville, still forty miles from Biondo, and Huston didn't meet them there either. When they finally caught up with him at the camp, Kate demanded again to talk about the script. His mind on guns and elephants, he put her off crossly, treating her as an interfering fussbudget. Gradually, though, she disentangled the director from her inadmissible anger at Tracy and grief over her mother and came to enjoy him. They had a lot in common.

The novelty of the camp charmed Kate into good humor again. She was pleased with her hut, which consisted of a bedroom and a porch, furnished with three benches, a bamboo table, and an army cot with a straw mattress, draped in mosquito netting. An electric lightbulb hung from the ceiling, supplemented by her flashlight. Out back was the jungle. She was going to live there for five weeks.

The local Africans, who had never seen a movie, were mystified by the whole enterprise. Kate was attended by her personal "boy," Tahili Bokumba, and they communicated with a few words of French. He did her laundry, cooked her solitary breakfasts, and hauled hot water to wash her silky hair that went limp in the humidity and had to live in paper curlers. She curried his favor with gifts of cigarettes. They smoked together in wordless comradeship.

With Humphrey Bogart in The African Queen.

At the "restaurant," a couple named van Thoms cooked for fifty people over wood fires and bottled gas, serving up most acceptable meals complete with wine. (Even in the tropics, Kate's appetite was awe-inspiring.) A monkey named Romulus made a nuisance of himself, biting people and stealing their drinks.

Toilet problems preoccupied Kate. The outhouse she was to share with the Bogarts was too intimate even to consider, so she resorted to the double boiler she'd bought in Stanleyville, lining the lower half with newspapers for ease in cleaning, popping the top half on, draping it with towels, and carrying it with her to empty on her way to the shower. She may be the only glamorous movie star ever to record such details for the world to read.

Rain poured down and delayed the shooting. An invasion of biting ants took over the huts, and Kate was covered with fiery welts, which luckily didn't show through her costume's long sleeves and high necks. When they were filming on the Ruiki River, mosquitoes, hornets, engine failures, and fouled propellers plagued cast and crew. The humidity was so dense that Kate had to keep her hat brim from drooping by dipping it regularly in rice water. The jungle served as toilet and dressing room. At one point *The African Queen*, the boat itself, actually sank and had to be hauled up, the mud shoveled out, and the motor repaired. But it was the first trip to Africa for everyone involved, every day was a novelty, and complaints were few.

For the next phase of filming, cast and crew pressed on to Lake Albert, where the houseboat *Lugard II* would take them to the foot of Murchison Falls. After a week or so onboard, all hands came down sick with vomiting, malaria, and diarrhea. Kate threw up everything she ate. As always, her favored cure was drinking floods of water, but in this case it was the wrong cure. The doctor had put everyone on bottled water, but they might have been better off drinking the river water or swilling whiskey like Bogart and Huston, who seemed to be immunized against the problem. The bottled water was heavily contaminated, and Kate, drinking more than anyone, was sicker than anyone. She had to switch to champagne, of which there was apparently plenty.

The sequences that called for immersion—the agonizing journey through the reeds, or Bogart fixing the propeller underwater—had to be shot in a tank in London, since no sane

John Huston was intensely excited about being in Africa. It triggered a manly fantasy in his inner ten-year-old, and for him the African experience was at least as absorbing as the job he'd come to do.

When filming at Biondo was finished, the cast, to its considerable relief, moved into a comfortable hotel in Entebbe, with golf, tennis, and hot and cold running showers. Most opted to rest up there for a few days before hitting the houseboat to Murchison Falls. Huston wanted to go on ahead at once and kill some game. Kate decided to go with him.

Producer Sam Spiegel was understandably horrified. He had a movie to make. Nothing could be done about his bullheaded director, but now his leading lady also wanted to go out and risk her life and his investment. He argued with her, appealing to her better nature, but she snapped back, "I want adventure. I want to hunt elephants with John. Not to kill, just to see." Spiegel sent Bogie to talk her out of it, but he had no better luck. "If you obey all the rules," she said, "you miss all the fun. John has fun."

She assured Bogie that she was a pretty good shot, and he warned her that Huston wasn't; he had an elegant, high-priced arsenal of guns, but he could barely hit a beer can. "If the elephant charges," Bogie said, "take my advice and run."

Kate was determined to drink the full African cup of adventure—if life offered you adventure, how could you say no? That night she replaced the buttons on Huston's trouser fly that had rotted off in the damp. In the morning they flew off, their plane flushing game from the jungle below.

They stowed their gear on the houseboat *Lugard II* and started out with a white scout, a black scout who wasn't allowed to carry a gun, and two bearers. Kate, always hungry, always thirsty, carried two shoulder bags full of water, biscuits, and bananas. Tracking the elephants by the flattened grass of their trail, led by a black tracker with a six-foot spear, they were stopped by "the most terrifying sound-noise-yell-screech." The elephants were downwind of them and had caught their scent.

The hunters circled prudently around the elephants, just as the sun came up, and then a large wild boar with her piglets trotting behind her crossed their path. Delighted, Kate cranked up her movie camera and started walking toward them, hoping for a closeup. A very quiet voice said, "Kate . . . come back, Kate." She stopped. "Come back, Kate—slowly." Kate backed up. The boar and her children moved harmlessly on.

Few wild animals are more dangerous than a boar with her young, and the impressive screeching of alarmed elephants was only a whisper of danger compared to Kate trying for a closeup of a very ugly customer indeed.

As the humid heat rose toward ninety degrees, they stumbled on a clearing with fifteen elephants gathered on a sort of family picnic. Huston yearned to shoot one. The hunting party crept up the hill, but the elephants, sensing trouble, melted away into the jungle.

"We'll go in after them," Huston said.

"No," said the white scout.

"You're just yellow," retorted the director, never a tactful man.

Kate tried to talk him out of it, but he persisted. Trained never to say no to risk, she followed him into the forest after the elephants for several hundred yards until, with an earthshaking roar, the herd crashed back past them, twenty or

JOHN HUSTON, DIRECTOR OF *THE AFRICAN QUEEN.*

thirty feet away, trees toppling in their path.

Huston was happy to have seen them charge. Kate was happy they were both still alive.

On the way back they shot an antelope for dinner, being in need of fresh meat, and, on the whole, Kate was pleased. Life had passed her the cup of adventure and she had not refused to drink. The years she had been cooped up caring for Tracy had been monotonously free of adventure.

person goes into an African river. The bilharzial parasite, for which there is no cure, creeps into the body's orifices; Kate remembered hearing of a silent-film actress, making a film in Africa, who went into a river and later died.

Kate had lost twenty pounds and was still sick when they got to London. Dr. Tom sent her a letter of introduction to the Queen's own physician and, slowly, she began to recover. Adventures can take their toll.

Some think *The African Queen* is her best movie. Her performance in *Long Day's Journey Into Night* was praised more highly by the critics, but surely *Queen*, based on a novel by C. S. Forester, is the best story. The battle of the sexes exploited in her comedies with Tracy pales beside the splendid tug-of-war between the prim but valiant spinster Rosie Sayer and the seedy, cautious Charlie Allnut. This time the balance between the two stars was perfectly calibrated and, though Kate always thought the ending was silly, the struggles and triumphs are splashed on a broader canvas than who-wears-the-pants-in-the-household.

For the generation in between her *Philadelphia Story* fans and her *On Golden Pond* fans, Katharine Hepburn will always be Rosie cheering as she and Mr. Allnut plunge down the murderous rapids, Rosie surfacing in the lake cheering after the homemade torpedo sinks the enemy ship. Now, there was a heroine a generation could sink its teeth into.

She was nominated for an Academy Award, but lost to Vivien Leigh in *A Streetcar Named Desire*. It was a good year in movieland.

When, still thin and wobbly, Kate got back to the United States to face the lurking reality of her mother's death, she found that her father had already remarried, to Madelaine Santa Croce, his longtime surgical nurse. The family banded together to accept her cheerfully, saying that Dr. Tom could hardly be expected to live alone and that it was splendid he'd have someone to look after him.

There was no way Kate could imagine criticizing her father. Still, she had always cherished her vision of her parents' utterly perfect marriage, and Dr. Tom's abrupt recovery may have come as a jolt, however staunchly she swore by the family tradition of jettisoning the past as soon as it happened.

After all, he could have hired a housekeeper.

circa 1952

CHAPTER EIGHT

BUSY ALL THE TIME

D on't forsake those duties which keep you out of the nut-house," Mrs. Hepburn had often said to her daughter. Kate, still exhausted from six months of dysentery, threw herself into work. Work was the only admissible treatment for grief, confusion, and perhaps dread of the clinical depression haunting her heredity.

Under her contract she had only one more movie to make for MGM, *Pat and Mike*, with Tracy, and then she was free. She filled her calendar: George Bernard Shaw's *The Millionairess* in London, then perhaps another movie with Huston, then *The Millionairess* on Broadway. This time she would be only four months in California with Tracy before setting forth again into her newly expanded world.

During her African jaunt Tracy gone back to drinking heavily and turned morose and reclusive, though not so reclusive that he didn't try to lure Joan Fontaine into his bed. Fontaine objected, citing Kate, and Tracy gave the classic Hollywood response that they were just good friends. Fontaine was firm; even so, he was a married man. Tracy replied, "I can get a divorce any time I want to, but my wife and Kate like things just as they are."

It may even have been true. Certainly Louise was spared the strain of caring for a moody, abusive drunk, and Kate, if she were married to Tracy, would hardly have felt she could use her new freelance status to roam the world.

She rented a house on Beverly Grove Drive (Howard Hughes made the arrangements; Kate had a talent for holding the friendship of ex-lovers), where she gave some dinner parties. While she was still secretive about her relationship with Tracy, she tried to normalize it with the small circle of friends

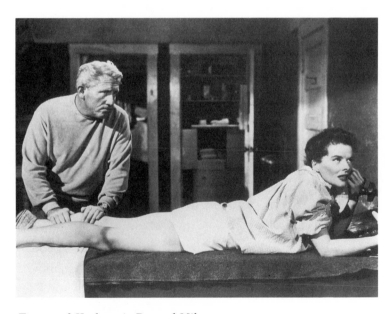

Tracy and Hepburn in Pat and Mike.

they cultivated—Cary Grant, Betsy Drake, the Bogarts, and the Garson Kanins.

Pat and Mike was yet another take on the same tired women-versus-men theme. (It's this one that contains Tracy's most famous line, "Not much meat on her, but what there is, is cherce.") Tracy here is a sports promoter who talks a gym teacher into seeking new horizons as a professional athlete under his management. The strenuous golf and tennis scenes got Kate into physical shape again, but emotionally she was cast back into her old role as Tracy's worshipful nurse/housekeeper.

The film was a popular and critical success, but it struck some people as odd, arriving in the movie houses so soon after *The African Queen*. A new and stronger actress had stormed onto the scene, to be quickly replaced by the old familiar foil for Tracy; which was the real Kate? If they were existing simultaneously, which would win the future?

Which indeed? Tracy sulked at Kate's plans. He had balked when Laurence Olivier, too, urged him to take up more challenges and broaden his considerable talents. He seemed immovable. He groused about an ulcer. He drank.

Kate, even while filming *Pat and Mike*, worked on *The Millionairess* script in every spare minute, and when the movie was wrapped she left Tracy for London. He began an affair with the actress Gene Tierney, his costar in *Plymouth Adventure*, perhaps hoping Kate would hear of it.

In London, Kate threw everything into *The Millionairess*. As had happened onstage before, her performance was dangerously manic. The play called for a jujitsu attack on her leading man, and she almost killed him. She screamed. She dashed around the stage in a frenzy. She broke a chair. She hit London like a thunderstorm, and audiences, feeling this must be an untamed American experience, loved it. So did critics. They called her a "hurricane" and a "tornado." One said the evening was like going over Niagara in a barrel. (Some carped that it was more an exhibition of personality than acting, but then, critics had often accused her of merely being Katharine Hepburn.)

Audiences queued up for tickets at five in the morning. Kate got crippling laryngitis that lasted for months. And in the middle of her hysterical efforts Tracy turned up in London with Gene Tierney, bent on sabotage as he had been during *Without Love*. He always enjoyed showing up to bedevil Kate when he wasn't expected and not showing up when he was.

Kate quivered on the edge of a nervous breakdown. She kept losing her voice and running mysterious fevers. Excused from matinees, she did manage to finish the play's run and fly back, exhausted, to New York, where she had promised the Theater Guild to do it all over again.

New York was less charmed than London. She was still having voice problems, and her apparently limitless energies were drained dry. Critics carped. *The New York Herald Tribune*'s Walter Kerr called her performance "razzle-dazzle" but "hollow." The possibility of suicide flickered through her mind. Whenever she could she slipped away to Fenwick to try to refill her spirits. For those who work to forget their problems, work can become as debilitating as drink. And those who need to see themselves as invincibly strong and healthy can quickly outrun their strength. With difficulty, she lasted the ten-week engagement.

Still keeping busy, she decided to adapt *The Millionairess* for film and star in it. She spent time, money, and energy on the project, but no studio would take it; it had never been one of Shaw's best stories. Kate was bitterly disappointed and frustrated, and at the same time had to have surgery for several skin cancers, an effect of the African sun.

The fateful fall into the canals of Venice in Summertime.

And always the demanding phone calls from Tracy; gloomy, paranoid, depressed, and needing reassurance, he interrupted her day and night. Though their relationship was going through rough times, he never lengthened her leash, and she never took a knife to it.

The offer to film *Summertime* in Venice for English director David Lean must have looked like a patch of blue sky in November.

Summertime was an amiable little project adapted from

Arthur Laurents's hit play *The Time of the Cuckoo*, dealing with a fortyish spinster schoolteacher who has saved up for years for a two-week vacation in Venice. (Hepburn's ravishing wardrobe by itself would have set a schoolteacher back decades of savings.) In Venice she falls in love with an antiques dealer, played by Rossano Brazzi, and all is sunsets and gondolas for a few days. But the Brazzi character is married, and the Hepburn character has to get home to her chalk and blackboards and her lonely future presumably brightened by memories.

The slapstick high point is when Kate falls into a canal. The canals of Venice are perhaps more lethal than the Ruiki River, sluggish with mud, garbage, and sewage, and Kate rebelled. Determined, Lean arranged to have a section of the canal barricaded with plastic and then treated with oceans of disinfectants. The resulting stew boiled up into unattractive suds. Kate, mindful of her recent skin-cancer surgery, backed away. The resourceful art director rigged up a team of propeller-like wind machines to drive the wave of foam away down the canal.

Kate, slathered with Vaseline, duly fell backward into the powerfully disinfected sewage. Lean wasn't satisfied. He made her do it again. And again. And again.

That night her eyes started to water. She had contracted a stubborn form of conjunctivitis that would never clear up. Those who were annoyed by her tearful close-ups in *The Lion in Winter*, finding them inappropriate for the great Eleanor of Aquitaine, would have been surprised to learn she couldn't help it. Having to act with tears in her eyes must have limited her approach and infuriated a woman who wanted always to be in charge of her body, but, being Kate, she never told the world and never complained.

Venice was less fun than anticipated. She was lonely and

worked long hours in the heat. Persistent rumors filtered in that Tracy was having an affair with the new Hollywood beauty, Grace Kelly. And John Ford, who had been collecting every scrap of news, every sighting of Kate since he came home from the war, tried to step back in.

If she was spending so much time away from Tracy, had Ford's time come around again? True, he had married Mary in the church; but he had been ill and suffered serious eye problems, and the hand of mortality had brushed him. Perhaps it wasn't too late to reach out for a taste of happiness. Seventeen years before, he and Kate had dreamed of Ireland and beginning a new life there. Kate and Ireland melted together in his mind. He made plans, to Mary's horror, to direct for an Irish film production company doing native Irish stories. Kate would come with him. She would be his star.

He wrote to Kate in Venice, but he had waited too long to make up his mind. Immediately she signed a contract with the Old Vic to tour Australia in *Measure for Measure*, *The Taming of the Shrew*, and *The Merchant of Venice*. She would be gone for six months. Why so far and for so long, no one can know. Perhaps the two men in her life were warring painfully in her mind, and the simplest solution was to run.

Both Ford and Tracy promptly hit the bottle. Ford drank so much directing *Mister Roberts* that he botched the picture. Tracy was so drunk and absent so often making *Tribute to a Bad Man* that MGM took him off the picture and canceled his contract.

Kate, in Australia enjoying the wildlife, the swimming, and the scenery (if not the tepid reception to her performances), heard all. Tracy was genuinely ill, though mostly through his own doing. The compulsive nursing reaction kicked in, and she came back to care for him. He had shortened her leash again.

In 1956 she was nominated for an Academy Award for *The Rainmaker*, though this movie belongs to her costar Burt Lancaster, who has a grand time hamming it up as Starbuck, a traveling con man. Passing through town to fleece the citizens, he convinces Lizzie, played by Hepburn in a severely repressive hairdo, that she's pretty. Her new self-esteem enables her to marry the deputy sheriff so she can wash his socks and iron his shirts. (Sometimes Kate's all-too-visible personality clashed with the temper of the times; in the 1950s, washing men's socks was a noble aspiration for a woman.)

The following year she and Tracy made *Desk Set*, a very light comedy about technology in the workplace. It wasn't one of their best, but audiences rejoiced to see the pair together after a five-year hiatus.

As always, her first concern was to cheer up the depressed and ailing Tracy and boost his confidence. In a move of amazing nerve she turned to Ford, the one man whose love for her

Desk Set, *1957.*

FORD, TRACY, AND THE LAST HURRAH

In 1958, Spencer Tracy and John Ford hadn't worked together for twenty-five years, during which time both of them had been deeply involved with the same woman. Ford was sixty-three and looked older, walking unsteadily, wearing an eye patch, and peering uncertainly through his damaged good eye. Tracy was fifty-seven and looked older, overweight and gasping with emphysema, white-haired and puffy from liver problems, his face seamed and his hands swollen. He showed up with no idea that Kate had engineered the assignment; she'd persuaded him that Ford needed him badly.

Both men were hypersensitive and wary. Both had been redheads, both were Irish binge drinkers with a strong need to dominate any situation. It could have been a disaster, but Ford obeyed Kate's instructions to the letter, offering little or no direction and plenty of praise and pretending to be exhausted by noon, so Tracy could get his nap. And there was no drinking. On St. Patrick's Day someone offered to bring in a case of Irish whiskey and Ford exploded with horror, claiming the whole place would shut down for a month. (His daughter, Barbara, counted eight known alcoholics on the set.)

Kate, who'd been touring in *Much Ado About Nothing*, showed up at the end of the first week to help baby-sit, but the tricky situation was running smoothly. As she had done while making *Mary of Scotland* with Ford, she served tea and biscuits on the set at four, and the strange triangle sat every afternoon chatting in a swirl of silent emotions. Sometimes the old affinity flared up between Ford and Kate. In private she called him Sean. Sometimes he reached out with kind offers that she greeted happily and then backed away from. Ford seemed to feel for Kate the same uncritical devotion that Kate felt for Tracy, and the contrast with Tracy's carping and sarcasm must have been vivid.

The Last Hurrah justified Kate's efforts. A clear hit, it broke Tracy's previous string of failures and reestablished his reputation and his ego. And Ford still dreamed of Kate in an Irish future.

she trusted. (How Ford would feel about it probably never entered her mind; to Kate, nobody's feelings counted for much beside Tracy's.) She asked him to cast Tracy as the Boston Irish mayor in *The Last Hurrah*. For her sake Ford, unlike other directors, would cosset Tracy and bolster his ego. Torn, Ford hesitated and kept changing his mind. Kate lobbied tirelessly. Finally Ford agreed, though it meant postponing the production, with considerable hardship all around, while Tracy finished the troubled *Old Man and the Sea*.

Relieved, Kate went east to do *The Merchant of Venice* and *Much Ado About Nothing* for Lawrence Langner. (Few Hepburn fans think of her as primarily a Shakespearean actress, but Garson Kanin says she did more Shakespeare than any other actress of her time—perhaps always with Mrs. Hepburn's opinion in mind.) While she was in the East, Tracy kept promising to visit her, but somehow never made it. Once she got as far as Idlewild (now Kennedy International) to meet him, but he wasn't on the plane; he had paused for a drink in Los Angeles and disappeared for days.

⬦ ⬦ ⬦

"Our greatest tragedienne"

In 1959, with the critical success of *The Last Hurrah* putting Tracy in better shape, Kate felt able to leave for London to film Tennessee Williams's macabre *Suddenly Last Summer*. She thought Williams was the country's best playwright; he thought she was every playwright's dream of an actress. Somehow, though, she wasn't happy. The homosexual theme was a first for the movies, but that can hardly have bothered Kate, friend of Noël Coward and Cole Porter. There was tension with her

Suddenly Last Summer, *1959.*

costars Montgomery Clift, who was falling apart psychologi-
cally, and his friend and champion Elizabeth Taylor, who had
to fight to keep him on. There was, for Kate, the novelty of
being cast and photographed for the first time as an old woman

next to the glamorous Taylor. And there may have been more. Biographer Leaming suggests that her role, a mother who refuses to accept the gruesome circumstances of her son's death and wants her niece lobotomized so she'll forget what happened, was a bit too close to the bone for Kate.

Kate was relieved to return to Tracy. To everyone's surprise *Suddenly* was a box-office as well as a critical hit and brought her another Academy Award nomination.

The next role came hard on its heels, as Kate played Mary Tyrone in the 1961 *Long Day's Journey into Night*, a heavyweight Eugene O'Neill drama. Tracy had been offered the splendid role of her husband but turned it down, saying the money wasn't good enough. He may have been simply being perverse; he may have felt he wasn't up to O'Neill.

Kate was, and the critics turned somersaults. This was the first time, they said, that Katharine Hepburn had played a part other than Katharine Hepburn. They seemed astounded by her unsuspected depth and insight. The notoriously brutal Pauline Kael of *The New Yorker* said she was now "our greatest tragedienne." Producers planned towering roles for her. She would play Sarah Bernhardt; she would play Queen Christina.

The public, on the other hand, wanted Hepburn to play Hepburn. *Journey*, acclaimed as her finest performance, is currently unavailable even from the mail-order video catalogs whose warehouses bulge with every conceivable filmed product.

And if at that moment Kate's future as a truly great dramatic actress lay spread before her, it was quickly rolled up and put away.

Both Tracy and Dr. Tom were seriously ill.

Once again, and at age fifty-five—well past the usual flowering time—Kate saw her world open up and then close again. Professionally, she vanished for the next five years.

On the set of A Long Day's Journey into Night.

Her patients had both fallen ill during the New York filming of *Journey*. She would drive to West Hartford after work on Friday to sit by her ailing father's bedside on Saturday, fly to California that night to help Tracy wrestle with his emphysema

LOUISE TRACY

In 1938, while Tracy was hiding in the hospital from the Academy Awards ceremony, his wife, Louise Treadwell Tracy, accepted his Best Actor award for *Captains Courageous* on behalf of her husband and children. She was dignified and gracious and the next day Ed Sullivan said in his column that she stole the show. "She is just the sort of person you expect Spencer Tracy's wife to be. Simple and unaffected."

Louise Tracy was, in the world's and her husband's eyes, a saint and a martyr. When her son John was born deaf, she dedicated herself to his care and education. Tracy, a man who needed great quantities of attention, felt neglected. The boy's problems left Spencer feeling helpless, guilty, and awed by his wife's patience.

Louise devoted the rest of her life to the deaf. She founded and directed the John Tracy Clinic for deaf children, based on working with their families to help them communicate. Tracy supported the clinic generously, and his name was on the letterhead, but he took no part in its doings. As Mrs. Spencer Tracy and its head, Louise was often in the news. She traveled and lectured and gave interviews, absorbed in her work. In 1956, when she won the Save the Children Foundation Award, the press hailed her as a great woman in the American humanitarian tradition. Four universities gave her honorary degrees.

She was much admired in the Hollywood world, though her social appearances were limited to fundraising for the clinic. And, uncomplaining through the decades of her husband's affair, she continued to take an intelligent interest in his career.

Her perfect behavior tortured Tracy with guilt. What man could divorce such a woman except with her blessing? She never gave it.

After Tracy died, Kate made contact with Louise. She offered help. She offered to be friends. Louise's odd response outraged her: "Well, yes," she said, "but you see, I thought you were only a rumor." "After nearly thirty years?" Kate snorted in retrospect. "Some rumor."

Thus did Louise Tracy have the last word, brushing aside what had been the center of Kate's life as mere gossip. She continued to be the publicly respected Mrs. Spencer Tracy until she died in 1983.

throughout Sunday, then fly back in time for work Monday morning. When the O'Neill film was finished, she was free to shuttle weekly between them for the next year.

Dr. Tom died in November 1962. He died as he would have wished, silently, teeth clenched against the pain, in full control till the end. Suffering from arteriosclerosis and a burst gall bladder, he succumbed at last to pneumonia. His death seems to have been less upsetting to Kate than her mother's had; perhaps it was overshadowed by worry over Tracy, or perhaps she had secretly never forgiven her father for his hasty remarriage.

Afterward, she flew back to Tracy's side, from which she would barely move for the rest of his life. Wings clipped, career abandoned, and energies stoppered up, she nursed her man. She was glad to.

In *Me*, she tells us severely that few people truly understand what's meant by "love." In her definition, love meant nothing less than total submission. You must give up everything you are or want for the loved one and expect nothing in return. Any crumbs that fall your way should be gratefully accepted, but never requested. She says simply, "I have no idea how Spence felt about me. I can only say I think if he hadn't liked me he wouldn't have hung around."

Was she right? Is this love's true face, or was she punishing herself for some secret crime? She tells us she loved doing it, that serving Tracy had made her deliriously happy every minute for nearly thirty years, but it's quite possible for the guilt-ridden to love punishment, and the punisher. Certainly, sensible therapists would shake their heads at such an unbalanced exchange. And certainly the rest of us, accustomed to a brisk and self-sufficient Katharine Hepburn, cringe at the vision of her on her knees before an ungrateful man.

On the other hand, there's something almost biblical in the

totality of her worship, especially after Dr. Tom's death. For her, Tracy was quite simply God, now the only God. If she had had a firstborn son, Tracy could have asked for his head.

Even ill as he was, Tracy wouldn't let Kate sleep in his little house. She would see to his comforts and then drive away alone. In her own bed, she would stay alert for the phone to ring.

She had let it be known she would accept work if Tracy could costar, but no studio offered. His emphysema made him as unreliable as his drinking once had, and he himself seemed to have lost interest. Perhaps turning down the O'Neill film had marked his mental retirement.

In the mornings, with Tracy asleep, Kate played tennis and visited John Ford in his office, or he would visit her in her rented hilltop house. He, too, seemed to be failing, and often spent days in bed, reading and smoking cigars. His eyesight and hearing were fading. He said he was tired. At home he and Mary squabbled bitterly about money. He begged Kate to make *7 Women* with him. He felt it would be his last picture and longed for her to be in it, but she couldn't leave Tracy.

In the afternoons, Kate might still take Tracy out for a drive, but there was always an oxygen tank on hand in case his breath gave out. When he collapsed from pulmonary edema at the beach house she'd rented one summer, she got him to the hospital in Los Angeles and then quickly disappeared, so that Louise, the very public Mrs. Spencer Tracy, could take charge and talk to reporters.

When he came back from the hospital he was so weak he allowed her to spend the nights in the maid's room, where she lay awake listening tensely for the sounds of his nightly routines, his prowling and his cups of tea for which she left a kettle on to simmer. After he improved, she moved out again, though she was always at his beck and call. When he was going to be away visiting Louise, she packed his lunch and dinner in a basket and put it on his doorstep.

Then Stanley Kramer, in a remarkable exhibit of faith, offered the pair the leads in *Guess Who's Coming to Dinner*. They would play the middle-aged couple whose daughter plans to marry a black man.

In 1966, the idea of interracial marriage was on the cutting edge of social conscience and must have tugged strongly at Kate's beliefs. Also she badly wanted Tracy to work again, for his ego's sake. In 1963 he had played a police captain in Kramer's *It's a Mad Mad Mad Mad World,* and his health had suffered from the desert heat, but this would be less taxing. Perhaps most persuasive of all, the movie would offer Kate's niece Katharine Houghton (Marion's daughter) a chance for her screen debut as the daughter. And just possibly, though she didn't say so, Kate herself wanted to work again.

Tracy resisted. He said he got too tired to do a day's work.

Tracy and Hepburn's final pairing, in Guess Who's Coming to Dinner.

Kate urged him, promising that he could quit every day at one o'clock. Kramer urged, too. He accused Tracy of sitting around waiting to die. Perhaps weary of arguing, Tracy caved in and, gasping and complaining, started work again.

It seemed as if he might not make it to the end. His emphysema kept him breathless, and his long final speech, which once he might have done in a single take, took six days to film. As usual Tracy worked out his frustrations on Kate, embarrassing the bystanders. "Christ, you talk like you've got a feather up your ass all the time."

After the final day's shooting, May 26, Tracy called all his friends in triumph; he'd made it all the way through.

Bad nights followed, though, and sometimes Kate lay on the floor by his bed until he seemed quiet, then tiptoed back to the maid's room to listen from there. In the small hours of June 10 she heard his footsteps, then a dropped cup breaking, and finally the sickening thump of a falling body. Spencer Tracy, age sixty-seven, had died of a heart attack.

Phone calls were made, and Louise Tracy, the widow, arrived to thrust Kate aside, take charge of arrangements, and give interviews to the press. It's unsurprising that Kate didn't join the family at the funeral mass, and even less surprising that she didn't join the throng at Forest Lawn Cemetery, where John Ford was the lead pallbearer and hundreds grieved. She had paid a private visit to Spencer's coffin at the undertaker's, and afterward, as was always her custom, she dealt with her feelings alone and out of the world's eye.

Guess Who's Coming to Dinner won Kate another Academy Award. She was upset that Tracy didn't win Best Actor, but told everyone that her award was really intended for the two of them. As usual, she hadn't seen the movie; she and Tracy had always avoided their finished films. To the viewer's colder eye, for perhaps the first time in his life, Tracy's performance lacks the force of personality, to put it mildly. He seems to wish he were somewhere else, perhaps home in bed with the door locked, and no doubt that's just what he wished.

Kate plays herself, warm but regal, and her "Well, I don't think I'm going to faint, but I'll sit down, anyway," is vintage Hepburn. The critics lapped it up, but slammed the film itself as hokum; thirty years later, it's embarrassing to watch. Sidney Poitier struggles with the portrayal of the Utterly Perfect Person. He's not just your average tall, dark, and handsome world-renowned professor of tropical medicine, he's also a natural winner, a man who strides to the airline baggage carousel and, in a single fluid motion, scoops up his briefcase and sweeps through the open door of the airport and into the open door of a taxi. He is kind but strong, thoughtful but decisive, passionate but chaste, loving but manly, and adores his parents.

As his fiancée, Kate's niece is cute as a button and good as gold, but a bit of a lightweight choice for a learned professor; the mismatch seems more intellectual than racial. The whole exercise is unfortunate, and it's a pity Tracy couldn't have left us after *Judgment at Nuremberg*.

Kate kept Tracy's cottage on Cukor's estate and stayed among the furnishings she'd arranged with such affectionate care. She managed to buy Tracy's old sports car, rich with memories, from Louise. But if her friends expected her to shrink from the world into grieving semiretirement, they were in for a shock. She was sixty years old, an age at which many actresses are forced to fade away, but she was just hitting her stride.

Either because, as always in grief, she wanted to keep busy, or because, released from her obsession, she was flooded with fresh energies, she plunged into work. Word got around that she was free again, offers came in, and she said yes.

circa 1982

CHAPTER NINE

THE FREEDOM YEARS

With no one to tug on her leash and no strings attached to her time and energy, Kate signed on for three new projects, two of which would keep her out of the country for a year. As Eleanor of Aquitaine in *The Lion in Winter*, she'd be filming in Wales, England, and France, and *The Madwoman of Chaillot* would be shot in the south of France. The third project was a challenge so new and almost bizarre that, being Kate, she couldn't say no. She was to play the French fashion designer Coco Chanel in Alan Jay Lerner's Broadway musical *Coco*, and become, in her sixties, a Hepburn who danced and sang and took an interest in clothes. She said she couldn't sing anything but "Onward, Christian Soldiers" (which she'd warbled valiantly in *The African Queen*) and promptly arranged for singing lessons.

Music had never meant much to Kate. It seemed a sort of

irritant, like perfume (which she also hated), and the racket of her New York neighbor Stephen Sondheim working on his brilliant *A Little Night Music* made her furious. Still, if she wasn't game for any dare, she wouldn't still be Hepburn. Her main worry over the musical was the prospect of wearing ladylike shoes without breaking an ankle.

She enjoyed making *Lion* and playing Eleanor, a tough bird who juggled not just men but entire countries. She may have been intrigued by the role of the wronged wife, having lived on the other side of that bed for so long. She also enjoyed teasing and bullying her costar Peter O'Toole on the set. Filming in Ireland, at Christmastime, she went swimming in the North

With Peter O'Toole in The Lion in Winter.

Atlantic. The shock was so awful, she explained cheerfully, that it made a person feel much better when it was over.

If Tracy's death had left her shattered, she gave no sign. Colleagues on the set remarked that she seemed much looser and freer, more like herself, with her old boss gone. Indeed, she was getting quite imperious without Tracy to slap her down.

Immediately after *Lion*, she was off for *Madwoman* in Nice, where she swam in the Mediterranean and, wearing an ancient red sweater of Tracy's, pedaled a borrowed bike through the hills.

Lion would win her another Oscar, but its glow was diminished by having to share it; in an unusual move the judges declared a tie and issued a second to Barbra Streisand for *Funny Girl. Madwoman*, in spite of a starry cast of luminaries like Danny Kaye, Yul Brynner, and her old flirt Charles Boyer, failed to gel and was rather a disappointment.

While *Coco* was held up with book problems, Kate and her friend Irene Selznick hatched a plan to make a movie about a young artist, based on a couple of books by British writer Margery Sharp, called *Martha in Paris*. Selznick, who had never produced a movie, would produce; Kate, who had never directed, would direct, leaving no challenge unmet. The fascinated screenwriter, James Prideaux, began taking notes for a book, *Knowing Hepburn*, not to be published until 1996, when she was past taking umbrage.

Then *Coco* got fixed and the Selznick project was shelved while Kate went to Broadway for her song-and-dance debut. She who for forty years had worn the same tan pants, black sweaters, white socks, and, for an accessory, a cigarette, would pretend to be a fashion designer.

Coco, in 1969, was the most expensive show in Broadway history, replete with mirrors, turntables, and special effects,

An original plays an original: Kate Hepburn on Broadway as Coco Chanel.

and it was a killing workout for its star, onstage almost every minute for its two and a half hours. In rehearsals, Kate's energy, fueled by constant munching on snacks of meat, fruit, cheese, and chocolates, left the younger cast members gasping by day's end. To keep up with the punishing routine and have wind enough to sing, Kate quit smoking. The cigarette of decades of photographs, as much a trademark as Churchill's cigar, was seen no more. This sacrifice didn't make her a singer, of course; Clive Barnes in *The New York Times* called her musical efforts a mix of "faith, love, and laryngitis." But Rex Harrison couldn't sing either, and it didn't hurt *My Fair Lady.* Kate talked her songs sincerely, like Harrison, and the audience knew that this was Hepburn herself, not Hepburn pretending to be a singer.

Her rather enigmatic brother Richard wore scarlet pajamas to opening night. Perhaps he felt it was time he got some of the world's attention.

The production was dazzling, almost too dazzling, an assault on the senses. To further discomfit the audience, Kate insisted on having all the theater's doors propped open to the winter night's fresh air. Huddled in overcoats, they loved her anyway. She claimed she could identify with Coco Chanel; but the audience identified her only with Hepburn, and that was fine with them. She had passed from being an actress, sometimes an antagonizing one, to a folkloric icon like, as she said herself, the Statue of Liberty.

Thanks to Kate's yeomanly efforts, this overwrought production ran for seven happy months, folding shortly after her replacement took over. John Ford, seventy-six and feeling every minute of it, made the taxing trip east to see *Coco*, or, rather, Kate. When he got home he wrote her a frank and touching love letter saying he'd come only to make his feelings about her perfectly clear.

Two days after he wrote the letter, he and his wife publicly celebrated their fiftieth wedding anniversary. When Mary was asked for the secret of her long marriage, she replied, "Believe nothing you hear and only half of what you see." Thus Mrs. Ford, like Mrs. Tracy, reduced Kate to a rumor and erased her from her husband's life. Perhaps if your husband was in love with Katharine Hepburn, the only way to cope was to pretend there was no Katharine Hepburn.

But Ford's trip had stirred up the old tenderness, and Kate began to stay in closer touch with her Sean. She wrote and called constantly. From Spain, where she'd gone as soon as she left *Coco* to film the Euripides drama *The Trojan Women*, she wrote him long, loving notes illustrated with drawings of her room, her view, the flora and fauna. (Why *The Trojan Women*? Because she'd never done a Greek tragedy before, she said, and she wanted to do everything—never mind how miscast she was as the woeful Hecuba, widowed Queen of Troy.)

Back home, she took *Coco* on tour. The touring production was actually better than the Broadway original, and certainly just as popular. Everywhere it played, fans cheered. As if Kate were the Grateful Dead, fans followed the show from town to town. Her long affair with Tracy was public knowledge now and seen as tragic and, on her part, quietly courageous. The mysterious long-burning loyalty to the idea of Hepburn had taken hold and was growing, all across geographic, social, and generational lines.

Plans to make a movie of *Coco* were scrapped. Kate worked long and hard on a screenplay of Graham Greene's *Travels With My Aunt*, but at the last minute the studio decided to use a younger woman (Maggie Smith was eventually cast in the role); Kate was dumped from the project without a cent. She made plans to sue but, never much interested in money, lost interest. For a frightening moment her calendar lay blank.

Arthritis was beginning to plague her. The tremors that she struggled to control gave rise to rumors of Parkinson's disease. (She always said the shakes yielded nicely to whiskey, though with too much whiskey everything else yielded, too.) In the East, she had her comfortable Turtle Bay house and garden, full of friends (and Luddy), and Fenwick, full of brothers and sisters (and Luddy) and her dear old canoe rigged with a sail. She was approaching seventy. She already had plenty of money and was so famous she could hardly walk down the street. Many people have happily retired to fewer lures. Something drove Kate to keep working.

In 1972, she jumped at the chance to play the mother in

Edward Albee's *A Delicate Balance*, maybe because it was to be filmed in London. She'd always loved London. She even stayed on in England, though she'd always sneered at television, to play Amanda Wingfield in David Susskind's television production of Tennessee Williams's *Glass Menagerie*. To her surprise, she thoroughly enjoyed the work, and the critics enjoyed her Amanda. (They said that occasionally she turned into Katharine Hepburn, but by now this was scarcely considered a flaw.)

When she got back to California she went to visit John Ford. She spent a week in the desert, near his ranch house, and came to sit and talk with him every day. He lay in bed, dying of cancer, a bottle of Guinness on the table and close at hand a bucket of the cigar butts he liked to munch on. They talked and talked, of themselves, each other, and Spencer Tracy, slowly stitching together the thirty-odd years of their loving separation. In another room, Mary Ford turned her radio up louder and pressed her lips together.

❦ ❦ ❦

"Goddamn, she's a great dame!"

Ford was dying, but Kate had many long miles left to go. George Cukor sent her the script of another television project, *Love Among the Ruins*, a comedy about an aging actress being sued for breach of promise by a younger man. It carried the promise of finally playing with Laurence Olivier (she was excited; he was wary). Unfortunately, at the crucial moment she had to have hip-replacement surgery and was ordered to

Finally matched with Olivier, in Love Among the Ruins.

rest for an indefinite period of time. There would be no Olivier film. Defiantly, she opted for the movie instead of the bed rest, and the surgeons were quite baffled by her recovery.

Cukor hired Tracy's daughter, Susie, to work as the still photographer on the project. So determined had Tracy been to keep his two lives separate that Kate had met her only once, and briefly. It must have been one of those moments described as awkward, but afterward the two became fairly friendly and were photographed comparing their remembrances of Tracy.

Ruins, with splendid sets and costumes, was a solid hit, and nobody suspected that the leading lady was supposed to be flat on her back in postoperative recovery. Like her father, she hated being bullied by pain.

And she hated the thought of age closing doors on her. Her sixty-eighth year found her galloping across deserts and shooting whitewater rapids in the Oregon outback, matching her endurance against John Wayne's. *Rooster Cogburn* was cobbled together as a combination sequel to Wayne's successful *True Grit* and a spinoff of Kate's successful *African Queen*, this time with a passel of murderers instead of a German ship to track down. It was a shamelessly commercial premise, but it brought together two of the most famous people on earth. "Duke" Wayne was the all-time top box-office draw; Katharine Hepburn, a record-breaking three-time Oscar winner. Between them, they had over three hundred screen credits.

The two hit it off at once. Kate thought Wayne was a real man, always her top compliment. Wayne, who called her "sister," thought Kate was a real woman, and tough, too. "Goddamn, she's a great dame!" he whooped. "She reminds me of me." Time by now had puffed and softened her face so she looked less austere and more lovable, and her eyes crinkled up when she laughed. And she and Wayne laughed all day, in the rugged Rogue River territory and Cascades forests where no portable toilets could be hauled in and the cast had to use the woods.

It wasn't a great movie, but it seems to have been fun to make.

Then Kate showered and changed and went back to Broadway to appear in Enid Bagnold's *A Matter of Gravity*. Once again, the theater critics were awed; her old fears of a possibly hostile live audience had sometimes driven her performances into hysteria, but fear would be absurd now. They loved her, and she knew it. She could relax.

The play would have run longer, but Kate stepped down after the scheduled twelve weeks and went off to dangle from the rope of a runaway hot-air balloon in the now-forgotten *Olly Olly Oxen Free*, playing a junkyard owner who helps two kids repair their balloon. The film is said to be a joy, but it never took off and has slipped out of sight.

Back on solid ground, she took *Gravity* on tour. Somewhere along the way she stepped into a hole and smashed her ankle and went on to perform in a wheelchair. Nothing except Spencer Tracy had ever been able to slow her down.

In the spring of 1977, *Gravity* closed in Phoenix, and Kate touched her bases at Fenwick and Turtle Bay. She swam, she cut firewood, she fed people well, sometimes bossily. She herself put away prodigious quantities of food all day and worried that guests and relations weren't eating enough. She dug and weeded in the Turtle Bay courtyard garden; neighbors invited friends over and passed out binoculars to watch the great Katharine Hepburn on her knees getting muddy.

Early in 1978, George Cukor, dear old friend and director, called. He was almost eighty and wanted to do one last film with her. The project he offered, a television production of Emlyn Williams's *The Corn Is Green*, would be filmed on location in Wales, and faraway places still sang to Kate. She loved the part of Miss Moffatt, a spinster teacher in the coal-mining country who offers to adopt the illegitimate baby of her favorite pupil so he can take up his Oxford scholarship. "Oh, indeed, a wonderful part," she told a friend later. "I laughed and I cried and cried. Lovely for me. A woman alive. Not half dead."

In truth, the play was dated and the searing shame of illegitimacy had, by the end of the 1970s, lost most if not all of its impact; but Kate had a grand time in Wales. She loped over the hills picking wildflowers and put on a gas mask to crawl 1,300 feet down into a mine tunnel to see what it was like down there. The only cloud was that she was required to ride an authentically massive, clunky 1890 bicycle over the steep muddy roads. She could manage on the level ground, but on the upgrades, for the first time, a stunt girl had to take over. Almost seventy, Kate could no longer do everything.

Having finished this final enterprise, George Cukor sold his estate, including the Tracy bungalow. Kate packed up her things there and moved them out, pulling up her last roots in California. From now on, home would be Fenwick and Turtle Bay—except when the siren call of work whistled her back.

Hollywood's grand old names had been falling away fast, and now the only two still working were Katharine Hepburn and Henry Fonda. *On Golden Pond* was inevitable. Oddly, living and working so long in such close quarters, the twain had never met, and when they were introduced, one or the other or perhaps both, depending on whose memory you trust, said, "Well, it's about time."

The tale concerns an affectionate couple, married for fifty years, at their summer house on a lake. Fonda's character is celebrating—if that's the right word—his eightieth birthday and, like Fonda himself, is failing fast. This downbeat material had trouble finding financing. Fonda's famous daughter, Jane, saved the day by lending her name, stepping in to play their visiting daughter, and acting as a coproducer.

The movie could have been purest treacle but saves itself

by intelligent dialogue, that rare and undervalued movie commodity. (The young screenwriter, Ernest Thompson, said he could simply have killed Kate for interfering, but she can't have done much damage; he won an Academy Award.) Fonda and Hepburn are sweet and salty with each other. Jane, who seems to have blown in from a different movie, plays the nightmare daughter from hell, a Californian mysteriously born to this reticent Yankee pair, who has avoided them for years because she feels that if her father had really loved her he would have said so more often. Happily, she leaves her elders and the movie early. Untangled by her departure, the plot is stripped down to an old man who doesn't want to die and the wife who loves him. It's wonderfully sufficient.

Reviewers yodeled with delight; *Time* magazine wrote, "There could have been trumpets, a heavenly choir. . . ." Only

On Golden Pond, *with Henry Fonda.*

a few critics carped at Kate for sentimentality, having no way to know that her welling tears were a souvenir of *Summertime* and that poisonous Venetian canal. Fonda, who died soon afterward, won his fifth Oscar, and Kate broke her own record with her fourth.

From the woods and waters of *On Golden Pond*, Kate headed straight back to the stage, because she'd been offered a new dare: learning to play the piano, as the aging concert pianist in *West Side Waltz*. She practiced for hours every day, getting the movements exactly right to fit the music. *Waltz* toured for nearly a year before opening on Broadway, where reviewers were cool to the play but warm to Kate's miraculous touch. When the play closed in New York she was seventy-five, but she went back on tour with it, cheerfully surviving the grueling theatrical life of late hours, hotel rooms, and constant travel.

Some might have considered a rest afterward, but Kate considered the film *The Ultimate Solution of Grace Quigley*, a black comedy about a little old lady arranging to have various folks who are tired of life relieved of its burden by a hit man. Apparently the fates were trying to slow her down, though, because that December, at Fenwick, she was speeding down an icy road and slammed into a utility pole. Her right foot was almost completely sliced off and hanging only by a tendon. She was rushed through the snow to Dr. Tom's Hartford Hospital, where the foot was miraculously reattached. After eight months back and forth to hospitals and six months of therapy, she was still in pain but more or less functional and went back to *Quigley*.

The death-to-order idea struck everyone as so bizarre that Kate had to raise the money herself. Raise it she did, though, and presently was once again frightening the executives, careening through the Bronx behind Nick Nolte on the back of a motorcycle. (Nolte called her "a cranky old broad who can sometimes be a lot of fun.") Nobody knew how painful the foot was or how much her back hurt. Like Dr. Tom, she never mentioned pain.

Quigley was not a hit. James Prideaux, the playwright who was still hoping to work with her, wrote, "She was shabby and dowdy and it was all about old people, not particularly ill or suffering, who killed themselves. . . ." When he asked her why she'd done it, she said, "It made me laugh." Nobody else laughed.

Nevertheless, she was finding fame useful and fun. Nobody said no to Katharine Hepburn. She was well taken care of always. Her aging, long-suffering secretary-companion, Phyllis Wilbourn, was still with her, still handling such boring details as money and plane tickets, like a faithful female Luddy. Kate's houses were always waiting to welcome her. Kate was queen of her world.

She'd grown unpredictable in public, able now to do as she pleased; she jaywalked, parked her car wherever it seemed convenient, legal or not, and said anything that popped into her mind.

When she was introduced to President George Bush, she looked him in the eye and said, "You're wrong about abortion. Why is that?"

"It's what I believe in," said the president.

Kate turned to Barbara Bush and asked, "Why do you put up with that?"

"Because I love him."

"I don't see how you could," Kate retorted.

James Prideaux wrote a television play for her, *Mrs. Delafield Wants to Marry*, about a woman who falls in love with

At the theater in New York, circa 1978.

a Jewish doctor, as seen through the eyes of a neighbor. CBS, also unable to say no to Kate, was delighted. *Delafield* aired on Easter 1986, with ratings that rejoiced hearts at CBS. Kate was nominated for an Emmy award, though she seemed vague about what that award might be.

She was busy. Louise Tracy being safely dead, Kate put together a ninety-minute PBS television documentary, *The Spencer Tracy Legacy: A Tribute by Katharine Hepburn*; half of Hollywood appeared in it, from Frank Sinatra to Tracy's daughter, Susie. Then, foraging for new fields to conquer, Kate wrote a screenplay called *Me and Phyllis* and tried hard to get it produced. Unfortunately it was so much "Me" and so little Phyllis that no actress could be found to take the meager second role.

Regretfully, Kate shelved that project and turned back to

Prideaux's new television play, *Laura Lansing Slept Here*, about an unwelcome, undeparting guest. The cast and crew set off for Vancouver, where they'd also filmed *Mrs. Delafield*. When they changed planes at O'Hare, Kate refused to sit down on the electric car trundling through the airport. She posed dramatically, standing on its bow, one foot up, staring ahead as "Washington Crossing the Delaware." Fellow travelers must have had trouble believing their eyes. Her father long ago had told her she wanted to be an actress only so she could show off in public; now, in her old age and full fame, she was free to show off blatantly, and she took pure delight in being the center of attention.

After Lansing, Kate went back to writing her memoir, *Me*. She wrote it reluctantly, almost resentfully. Much as she wanted another best-seller to follow her *African Queen* memoir, which was published in 1987, this one ran against the grain. Where Kate came from, self-analysis was considered unwholesome and self-indulgent; the past was to be buried as quickly as possible. Perhaps all roads into the past led inexorably to that morning in the attic in New York when she was thirteen.

Me is a curious read, written in a childishly breathless style full of dashes, like a postcard scribbled in haste. She rushes up to people and events, deals them a glancing blow, and skitters away. She's careless with facts and dates, as if too rushed to check them; she lingers over the trivial and brushes off the solid. For all her famous arrogance, there's a kind of modesty here, as in "who would want to know how I really felt?" Or perhaps it's just the same reflexive privacy that led her to hide her birthday even from her closest friends, even from her passport.

Basically what she tells us, over and over, is how happy, loved, and lucky she's been. Nobody, considering the known facts of her life, would reach the same conclusion, but Kate looks back into blinding sunshine. Bad luck and sorrows would have been shameful, a kind of failure, so Kate walks backward through her past lighting candles wherever there might be darkness.

In her eyes, even her career was effortless. When Prideaux remarked to her how tough an acting career is, Kate snapped, "Not for me. I had it all handed to me on a silver platter." She didn't, but never mind.

Me was indeed a best-seller; and when *Lansing* aired on television, the whole world watched, and Kate was buried under fan mail. She wanted to do another television play, and Burt Reynolds declared it was his lifelong dream to act with her. (From John Barrymore to Burt Reynolds was a long, long road.) But then Reynolds backed out for a different project, and Prideaux had overdosed on Hepburn.

Receiving an honorary doctorate at Columbia University, 1992.

At eighty-five, her career was winding down.

The actress and director Elaine May told Garson Kanin how deeply she admired Hepburn: "She really is about the only person who gives you the feeling that maybe it could be a woman's world." She was the one feminist hero admired equally by men and the unpoliticized young. Something about her spoke to everyone. Probably few Elvis Presley fans wanted to be Elvis, but all Hepburn fans want to be just a little like Hepburn— stand up a bit straighter, welcome more risks, laugh more, and take longer strides through life.

John Bryson, who adored her, wrote, "Mean as a snake, dear as an angel, she is one of the great humans, better than the legend. She is all that she appears to be, with a face for Mount Rushmore."

She went on and on. In *African Queen*, in the domestic doldrums of the '50s when marriage was a woman's only proper goal, Kate had made "Miss" a respectable name to be called. In the '80s, she made "old lady," for the first time in modern history, a term meaning vigorous, spirited, strong, and independent. Always independent. She had loved like a woman, but she lived like a man.

When, in 1971, *McCall's* magazine named her their first Woman of the Year, they defended their choice by saying she had "the traditional feminine virtues in untraditional ways. . . . Her grace is in her gallantry, her sure sense of self."

She never let us down. She never went sodden with drugs or drink and never whined. She left the grand Tracy love story intact for us and never took up serial husbands. For all her eccentricities and feistiness, she was a perfect lady to the last.

In October 1996, a supermarket tabloid ran a story on Kate, who had just pulled through another health crisis. An unnamed "family insider" reported that, just as everyone

HEARTY BREAKFASTS, ICY PLUNGES

Kate once told Garson Kanin, "A good life is a collection of good habits, and the other way about." Kate's good habits, pursued into her eighties, echoed her father's early demanding routines and might have killed a lesser mortal. She believed, for instance, that the only cure for the common cold was a good swim in northern seawater, the icier the better. Pushing the limits of physical endurance, she exhausted anyone trying to keep up. She had to abandon her regular golf games, finally, when her back gave out, but she took up skateboarding and went on playing tennis, defying her arthritis, the pain in her shattered ankle, and the increasing tremor in her neck and hands.

At Fenwick, she still rose before dawn, washed her hair and wrapped it in a towel, built a fire, made herself breakfast—bacon, chicken livers, steak, eggs, a jug of orange juice, and a pot of coffee—and took it back to bed, where she ate and watched the sun rise. In New York, she took long walks through Central Park's most dangerous places; what mugger would lay a hand on Katharine Hepburn?

The photographer John Bryson, who'd been a friend since *Rooster Cogburn*, visited often at both her houses, taking pictures of Kate at work and at play, Kate on location for movies, Kate cooking, Kate in her canoe with its homemade-looking sail, Kate chopping firewood in Connecticut and unloading it in New York. When the windchill factor was twenty below zero, Bryson gamely bundled up and took pictures of her morning swim in ice-fringed Long Island Sound. ("Not everyone," she told him, "is lucky enough to understand how delicious it is to suffer.")

In the end her healthy habits may have served her badly and kept her around a little longer than she would have wanted. In spite of decades of steaks and cigarettes, she lived on beyond her independence. She lived to use a walker, need a nurse, and watch her memory fade, though always her sharp, self-deprecating wit and iron will gleamed through.

circa 1994

thought it was over, she regained consciousness and said, "I'm not gone yet. You can't get rid of me that easily." The source goes on to report the details of the funeral she'd planned for herself, right down to the music (*Rhapsody in Blue*) and the menu (New England clam chowder and lobster).

Two months later another tabloid ran a cover story reporting her failing health and memory: BRAVE KATE'S LAST DAYS. She shares the cover with two younger celebrities: DI SLAPS FERGIE IN CATFIGHT OVER LOVE SECRETS.

The reader, idling in the checkout line, might well conclude that standards of behavior among popular heroines aren't what they used to be when Katharine Hepburn was queen.

CHRONOLOGY

1907   November 8 (May 12 in other sources): Born in
Hartford, Connecticut

1912   Hepburn family purchases the Fenwick House and
begins spending summers on Long Island

1921   Spring: Brother Tommy hangs himself

1924   Fall: Enrolls in Bryn Mawr

1927   April: Makes college stage debut as Oliver in *The
Truth About Blayds*

1928   Play: *The Woman in the Moon* (at Bryn Mawar)
Meets Ludlow Ogden Smith, a.k.a. "Luddy"
Graduates from Bryn Mawr with honors
Meets Phelps Putnam
December 12: Marries Luddy
Plays: *The Big Pond* (for one performance), *These
Days*, understudies in *Holiday*, *The Czarina*, *The
Cradle Snatchers*

1929   Play: *Death Takes a Holiday*

1930   Plays: Understudies in *A Month in the Country*, *Art
and Mrs. Bottle*, *The Admirable Crichton*, *The
Romantic Young Lady*, *Romeo and Juliet*

1931   Plays: *The Animal Kingdom*, *Just Married*, *The Cat
and the Canary*, *The Man Who Came Back*

1932   Lands RKO contract and goes to Hollywood
       Meets Leland Hayward and begins affair
       Completes her first film—*A Bill of Divorcement*
       Plays: *The Warrior's Husband, The Bride the Sun
       Shines On*
1933   Earns her first Academy Award for *Morning Glory*
       Films: *Christopher Strong, Morning Glory, Little
          Women*
       Play: *The Lake*
1934   April: Travels to Mexico and files for divorce from
          Luddy
       Films: *Spitfire, The Little Minister*
1935   Films: *Break of Hearts, Alice Adams*
1936   Begins relationship with director John Ford while
          making *Mary of Scotland*
       Films: *Sylvia Scarlett, A Woman Rebels, Mary of
          Scotland*
       Play: *Jane Eyre*
1937   Meets Howard Hughes and moves onto his estate
       Films: *Quality Street, Stage Door*
1938   Films: *Bringing Up Baby, Holiday*
1939   Play: *The Philadelphia Story*
1940   Films the screen version of *The Philadelphia Story*
          and earns an Academy Award nomination for
          Best Actress
1941   August: Katharine Hepburn and Spencer Tracy meet
1942   Makes her first movie with Spencer Tracy—*Woman
          of the Year*
       Receives another Academy Award nomination for
          Best Actress
       Film: *Keeper of the Flame*
       Play: *Without Love*

1943   Film: *Stage Door Canteen*

1944   Film: *Dragon Seed*

1945   Film: *Without Love*

1946   Film: *Undercurrent*

1947   Films: *The Sea of Grass, Song of Love*

1948   Film: *State of the Union*

1949   Film: *Adam's Rib*

1950   Mother, Kit Houghton Hepburn, dies

         Goes on tour in her first Shakespearean lead,
            Rosalind, in *As You Like It*

1951   Travels to Africa to film *The African Queen* with
            Huston, Bogart, and Bacall

1952   Film: *Pat and Mike*

         Play: *The Millionairess*

1955   Film: *Summertime*

         Plays: On tour in Australia with *The Taming of the
            Shrew, Measure for Measure, The Merchant of
            Venice*

1956   Films: *The Rainmaker, The Iron Petticoat*

1957   Film: *Desk Set*

         Plays: American Shakespeare Festival: *The Merchant
            of Venice, Much Ado About Nothing*

1959   Earns Academy Award nomination for Best
            Actress for her work in *Suddenly Last Summer*

1960   Plays: *Twelfth Night, Antony and Cleopatra*

1962   November: Dr. Tom Hepburn, Katharine's father, dies

         Long Day's Journey into Night produces yet another
            Best Actress nomination

1966   June 10: Spencer Tracy dies at the age of sixty-seven
            of heart attack

1967   Hepburn and Tracy's last film together—*Guess
         Who's Coming to Dinner*—is released

Hepburn receives Academy Award for Best Actress

1968   Her performance in *The Lion in Winter* produces her third Academy Award

1969   Debuts in first Broadway musical—*Coco*

Film: *The Madwoman of Chaillot*

1971   Film: *Trojan Women*

1973   *The Glass Menagerie* marks her television debut

1974   Television: *A Delicate Balance*

1975   Television: *Love Among the Ruins*

1976   Play: *A Matter of Gravity*

1978   Film: *Olly Olly Oxen Free*

1979   Television: *The Corn Is Green*

1981   Pairs up with Henry Fonda in *On Golden Pond* and earns her fourth Academy Award for Best Actress

Play: *West Side Waltz*

1984   Film: *The Ultimate Solution of Grace Quigley*

1986   Puts together a PBS documentary *The Spencer Tracy Legacy: A Tribute by Katharine Hepburn*

Earns an Emmy nomination for *Mrs. Delafield Wants to Marry*

1987   Publishes her memoir—*The Making of The African Queen, or, How I Went to Africa with Bogart, Bacall, and Huston and Almost Lost My Mind*

1988   Television: *Laura Lansing Slept Here*

1991   Publishes her second autobiography, *Me: Stories of My Life*

1994   Film: *Love Affair*

BIBLIOGRAPHY

BOOKS

Andersen, Christopher. *Young Kate: The Remarkable Hepburns and the Childhood That Shaped an American Legend*. New York: Henry Holt, 1988.

Bergan, Ronald. *An Independent Woman*. New York: Arcade Publishing, 1996.

Bryson, John. *The Private World of Katharine Hepburn*. Boston: Little Brown, 1990.

Edwards, Anne. *A Remarkable Woman*. New York: Morrow, 1985.

Deschner, Donald. *The Films of Spencer Tracy*. New York: Citadel Press, 1993.

Hepburn, Katharine. *The Making of The African Queen, or, How I Went to Africa with Bogart, Bacall, and Huston and Almost Lost My Mind*. New York: Knopf, 1987.

———*Me: Stories of My Life*. New York: Knopf, 1991.

Kael, Pauline. *Kiss Kiss Bang Bang*. New York: Little Brown, 1968.

Kanin, Garson. *Tracy and Hepburn*. New York: Viking, 1971.

Leaming, Barbara. *Katharine Hepburn*. New York: Crown Publishers, 1995.

Prideaux, James. *Knowing Hepburn and Other Curious Experiences*. New York: Farber and Farber, 1996.

PERIODICALS

Journal-American
National Enquirer
National Examiner
New York Times
Newsweek
The New Yorker
Time

FILMS

Guess Who's Coming to Dinner. Columbia Pictures, 1967
Morning Glory. RKO, 1933
Pat and Mike. MGM, 1952

SOURCES

CHAPTER ONE

REFERENCES

Andersen; Bryson; Leaming; Hepburn: *Me: Stories of My Life*.

SOURCES

p. 4 *"Never forget that they"*: Bryson, p. 107.

p. 4 *"I was always playing"*: ibid, p. 136.

p. 5 *"I've had a pretty remarkable"*: Andersen, p. 14.

p. 7 *She never told her brother-in-law*: ibid, p. 30.

p. 8 *"a divine command"*: Leaming, p. 38.

p. 13 *"he found moaning"*: Hepburn: *Me: Stories of My Life*, p. 56.

p. 14 *"more of a sitter"*: Leaming, p. 97.

p. 14 *"If I don't marry"*: ibid.

p. 17 *"Just use any of them"*: Bryson, p. 37.

CHAPTER TWO

REFERENCES

Andersen; Hepburn: *Me: Stories of My Life*; Leaming; *A Social History of the American Family*.

SOURCES

p. 21 *"the thunderous voice"*: Leaming, p. 138.

p. 22 *"The girl must be allowed"*: *A Social History of the American Family*, vol. 2, p. 114.

p. 22 *"Then I can have a baby"*: Leaming, p. 138.

p. 22 *"unless perhaps I can find"*: Andersen, p. 203.

p. 22 *"They brought us up"*: Hepburn: *Me: Stories of My Life*, p. 27.

p. 23 *"Were we spanked?"*: Andersen, p. 128.

p. 23 *"You were just supposed"*: ibid.

p. 28 *"Well, fine, Kit"*: ibid.

p. 29 *"You're my favorite girl"*: Leaming, p. 190.

p. 29 *"asphyxia by hanging"*: Hepburn: *Me: Stories of My Life*, p. 46.

p. 30 *"simply did not believe"*: Leaming, p. 194.

CHAPTER THREE
REFERENCES
Andersen; Edwards; Hepburn: *Me: Stories of My Life*; Leaming.
SOURCES
p. 38 *"He did not seem to"* and ensuing: Edwards, p. 46.

p. 38 *"complete satisfaction of"*: Leaming, p. 256.

p. 38 *"an odd-looking"*: Hepburn: *Me: Stories of My Life*, p. 90.

p. 38 *"the soul of sensitivity"*: ibid, p. 92.

p. 40 *"You just want to"*: Andersen, p. 247.

p. 40 *"thought acting was"*: Hepburn: *Me: Stories of My Life*, p. 81.

p. 41 *He was not going to change*: Andersen, p. 22.

p. 41 *"had talent and"*: Hepburn: *Me: Stories of My Life*, p. 81.

p. 42 *"there didn't seem to be"*: ibid, p. 94.

p. 44 *"How are you feeling"*: Leaming, p. 258.

p. 44 *"If you want to sacrifice"*: Edwards, p. 46.

CHAPTER FOUR
REFERENCES
Andersen; Bergan; Edwards; Hepburn: *Me: Stories of My Life*; *Journal-American*; Leaming; *Morning Glory*, Turner Home Entertainment; *New York Times*.

SOURCES

p. 47 *"What am I doing"* and ensuing: Leaming, p. 260.

p. 49 *"like a death's head"*: Hepburn: *Me: Stories of My Life*, p. 109.

p. 49 *"galumphing there like"*: Edwards, p. 49.

p. 50 *"Nobody with your vicious"*: ibid, p. 57.

p. 50 *"Get me a bowl of"*: Leaming, p. 268.

p. 51 *"the most appalling and"*: Edwards, p. 67.

p. 51 *"like a cross between"*: Bergan, p. 9.

p. 53 *"If you didn't get it right"*: Andersen, p. 195.

p. 53 *"Of course I did it"*: Edwards, p. 74.

p. 53 *"She is so real"*: Leaming, p. 274.

p. 54 *"And it wasn't long"*: Hepburn: *Me: Stories of My Life*, p. 183.

p. 56 *"I disobey rules that"*: Andersen, p. 16.

p. 57 *"kind of power that"*: *New York Times*, December 9, 1937.

p. 59 *"a valuable piece"*: *Morning Glory*, Turner Home Entertainment.

p. 59 *"I'm not afraid!"*: *New York Times*, December 9, 1937.

p. 59 *"cinema's wonder girl"*: Leaming, p. 282.

p. 61 *"She ran the gamut"*: *Journal-American*, December 27, 1933.

CHAPTER FIVE

REFERENCES

Bergan; Bryson; Edwards; Hepburn: *Me: Stories of My Life*; Kanin; Leaming; *The New Yorker*; *Time*.

SOURCES

p. 65 *"and all she ever"*: *The New Yorker*, November 11, 1996.

p. 67 *"Katharine Hepburn is"*: *Time*, January 1936.

p. 67 *"she was a bit of"*: Hepburn: *Me: Stories of My Life*, p. 235.

p. 70 *"You're a fine girl"*: Leaming, p. 316.

p. 71 *A niece of Ford's*: ibid, p. 329.

p. 74 *"We had a very"*: Hepburn: *Me: Stories of My Life*, p. 199.

p. 75 *"He is part of the family,"*: ibid, p. 200.

p. 75 *"Miss Hepburn really is"*: Edwards, p. 130.

p. 78 *"Hepburn has two strikes against"*: Bergan, p. 9.

p. 82 *"like a woman who has"*: Leaming, p. 371.

p. 83 *"You're rather short"* and ensuing: Kanin, p. 4.

p. 83 *"I'm afraid I'm"* and ensuing: Edwards, p. 159.

p. 83 *"I hope it doesn't bother you"*: Bryson, p. 118.

CHAPTER SIX
REFERENCES
Bryson; Edwards; Kanin; *Time*.
SOURCES

p. 85 *"Imagine how she must"*: Bryson, p. 175.

p. 85 *"magical for both of us,"*: ibid, p. 127.

p. 90 *"worst bunch of shit"*: ibid, p. 133.

p. 90 *"succeed in turning several"*: Kanin, p. 145.

p. 90 *"Nobody's better than when"*: Edwards p. 167.

p. 92 *"I could hear every"*: Kanin, p. 42.

p. 96 *"with the same man"*: *Time*, January 1942.

p. 97 *"Well, you know Madam"*: Kanin, p. 50.

p. 99 *"I don't own one damned"*: ibid, p. 208.

p. 99 *"I've lived like a man."*: Edwards, p. 185.

p. 104 *"the best actor I've"*: Kanin, p. 108.

p. 104 *"no bullshit in it . . ."*: Bryson p. 66.

p. 104 *"more than an actor"*: Kanin, p. 37.

p. 105 *"You're not going to tell me"*: ibid, p. 149.

CHAPTER SEVEN
REFERENCES
Edwards; Hepburn; Kanin; Leaming.
SOURCES

p. 110 *"more showmanship than"*: Leaming, p. 437.

p. 110 *"strident insistency"*: ibid.

p. 110 *"longtime admirer of this"*: Leaming, p. 437.

p. 113 *"I'm throwing away"*: ibid, p. 442.

p. 114 *"What you do is to"*: Edwards, p. 207.

p. 114 *"studied old-Kentucky-colonel"*: Hepburn, p. 10.

p. 115 *"Yes," she said, "but I've"*: Kanin, p. 74.

p. 116 *"everyone focuses attention"*: ibid, p. 13.

p. 117 *"I gazed at her and"*: Hepburn, p. 34.

p. 120 *"I want adventure"* and ensuing: Hepburn, p. 92.

p. 120 *"If the elephant charges"*: ibid, p. 93.

p. 120 *"the most terrifying"*: ibid, p. 95.

p. 121 *"Kate...come back, Kate"*: ibid, p. 96.

p. 121 *"We'll go in after"* and ensuing: ibid, p. 98.

CHAPTER EIGHT

REFERENCES

Deschner; Edwards; Hepburn: *Me: Stories of My Life*; Kael; Leaming;
  MGM.

SOURCES

p. 125 *"Don't forsake those"*: Hepburn: *Me: Stories of My Life*, p. 224.

p. 126 *"I can get a divorce"*: Edwards, p. 271.

p. 127 *"Not much meat on"*: *Pat and Mike*, MGM, 1952.

p. 127 *They called her a "hurricane"*: Edwards, p. 224.

p. 128 *"razzle-dazzle"*: Leaming, p. 459.

p. 133 *His daughter, Barbara*: ibid, p. 477.

p. 136 *"our greatest tragedienne."*: Kael, p. 298.

p. 138 *"She is just the sort"*: Deschner, p. 47.

p. 138 *"Well, yes," she said, "but"*: Hepburn: *Me: Stories of My Life*,
  p. 407.

p. 139 *"I have no idea how"*: ibid, p. 396.

p. 142 *"Christ, you talk"*: Leaming, p. 492.

p. 143 *"Well, I don't think"*: *Guess Who's Coming to Dinner*, Columbia Pictures, 1952.

CHAPTER NINE

REFERENCES

Bryson; Kanin; Leaming; *National Enquirer*; *National Examiner*; *New York Times*; *Newsweek*; Prideaux.

SOURCES

p. 148 *"faith, love, and laryngitis"*: *New York Times*, December 19, 1969.

p. 149 *"Believe nothing you"*: Leaming, p. 503.

p. 150 *She always said*: Bryson, p. 88.

p. 153 *"goddamn, she's a great"*: ibid, p. 58.

p. 154 *"Oh, indeed, a wonderful"*: ibid, p. 74.

p. 156 *"There could have been"*: Bryson, p. 135.

p. 158 *"a cranky old broad"*: *Newsweek*, November 1983.

p. 158 *"She was shabby and"* and ensuing: Prideaux, p. 126.

p. 158 *"You're wrong about"* and ensuing: ibid, p. 255.

p. 161 *"Not for me. I had"*: Prideaux, p. 79.

p. 162 *"She really is about"*: Kanin, p. 230.

p. 162 *"Mean as a snake,"*: Bryson, p. 49.

p. 162 *"the traditional feminine"*: Kanin, p. 79.

p. 163 *"A good life is a"*: ibid, p. 69.

p. 163 *"Not everyone,"*: Bryson, p. 49.

p. 164 *"I'm not gone yet"*: *National Enquirer*, October 15, 1996.

p. 165 *"BRAVE KATE'S"* and ensuing: *National Examiner*, December 3, 1996.

PHOTOGRAPHY CREDITS

INDEX

ABOUT THE AUTHOR

Barbara Holland is a freelance writer whose work has appeared in *The Washington Post*, *Smithsonian*, *Ladies Home Journal*, *Good Housekeeping*, *Country Journal*, and *Women's Day*, among others. Her books include *Bingo Night at the Fire Hall* and *Endangered Pleasures*. She lives in Belmont, Virginia.